A
Second
View of
Things:
A Memoir

Albert W. Trueman

A
Second
View of
Things:

A Memoir

McClelland and Stewart

McClelland and Stewart Limited
The Canadian Publishers
25 Hollinger Road
Toronto, Ontario
M4B 3G2

Financial assistance of the Ontario Arts Council toward the
publication of this book is gratefully acknowledged.

Canadian Cataloguing in Publication Data

Trueman, Albert W. (Albert William), 1902-
   A second view of things

ISBN 0-7710-8638-5

1. Trueman, Albert W. (Albert William), 1902-
2. Universities and colleges - Canada - Administration - Biography. 3. Arts administrators -
Canada - Biography. I. Title.

LA2325.T78A3   378'.111   C82-094623-0

Printed and bound in Canada

For Jean and Peter and Sally

ACKNOWLEDGEMENTS

Whatever merits this book may have are due in large measure to my wife, who read it as I produced it, exercised her considerable critical judgment upon it, urged upon me certain refinements of expression, and encouraged me "to put it all down"; to Professor George B. Johnston, colleague at Carleton University, poet, "a dear, a true industrious friend," who spurred me on to write the book and has criticized the product with utmost candour, good will, and marvellous sympathetic patience; and to my son, Peter, who lived with these pages as I wrote them, chapter by chapter, and never failed to cheer me on.

INTRODUCTION

Canada does not have a rich store of autobiography. The deficiency is marked in those areas that do not ordinarily arouse sustained public curiosity – higher education, scholarly research, the administration and development of the arts. Politicians who achieve office, whether or not they write autobiographies or keep diaries, are assured of contemporary recognition and the eventual concern of historians. But educators, scholars, and heads of cultural institutions rarely emerge into public view, either during their lives or afterwards. No doubt they welcome this anonymity, especially during their active careers. But the result is a gap in the record, a national amnesia in cultural history, so that, ignorant of the past, Canadians live in a perpetual daze of newness. Autobiographies of those who worked in these areas are thus particularly valuable, for they give substance and a human glow to what, otherwise, would be a thin and uninviting record. We are grateful that Albert Trueman ignored the advice of a young friend – "*Don't* write your memoirs!" – and set down carefully and lovingly his recollections of a long, varied, and important career.

In the 1940's and 1950's, whenever there was a crisis or a new departure in the educational life of the nation, there was an insistent call for the services of Albert Trueman; and he answered the call with a frolic welcome. He was twice a University president: at Manitoba, where he struggled with an impossible administrative structure; at New Brunswick, where he learned to live with the demanding benevolence of Lord Beaverbrook. He was a University Chancellor, who helped the President to restore harmony and direction. He was Chairman and Commissioner of the National Film Board when it was in the painful process of adjusting to profound changes. Most impor-

7

tant, he was the first Director of the Canada Council, who contributed in major ways to shaping the policies that have given the Council stability and a central place in our cultural life. This long, tough administrative career was preceded and followed by two lengthy and joyful periods of teaching in the University.

This autobiography is thus an important public record. It is also, as every autobiography should be, part confession, part apologia; in short, a self-portrait. When he first talked to me about writing his autobiography, he thought of calling it *No Enemy, but Winter and Rough Weather*. The title, as I feared, did not survive: it was too long, and, for non-Shakespeareans, would have aroused confused and irrelevant associations. But it accurately reflected the spirit in which he was writing the book. He is buoyant about his career – packed with problems and irritations, carrying its share of disappointments, but, seen as a whole, happy and satisfying. He has a relish for human beings; there are no sinister villains in his reading of events (with one possible exception); words by others uttered in anger he forgets and forgives.

Although an autobiography is highly personal, there is a limit to self-portraiture. It is difficult for the writer to see himself as others see him. I, therefore, offer this portrait: Albert Trueman was a tall man, with a commanding physical presence, measured and a little formal in speech, but without pomposity. He had a deep, resonant voice that he used on the public platform with calculated dramatic effect, hinting at the operatic career that he might well have had. He was a genial and witty companion, given occasionally to bouts of hamletian self-analysis, from which he would rapidly emerge with renewed vigour and undiminished joviality. He took satisfaction in the honours he had received – honorary degrees from a number of universities and membership in the Order of Canada — but he rejoiced most in the love that encompassed him in his family and in the affectionate esteem in which he was held by friends and colleagues everywhere.

He is now officially retired from all duties, but the portrait needs no revision, except to add that his vigour, congeniality, and wide interests are undiminished.

CLAUDE BISSELL

FOREWORD

Shortly after it was announced that I was retiring from the University of Western Ontario, in 1967, I went to a party given by the Trottiers: Gerald Trottier was then Resident Artist at Western. A young London painter, Ronny Martin, said to me, "I hear you're retiring, Doc." He put his hand on my sleeve and said, "*Don't* write your memoirs!" This piece of gratuitous advice in a way has inhibited me for years. But I have often thought that I wanted to write something; something about the way the years have treated me, a record of what has been an exciting and very, very, lucky life, lived in Canada since I was eleven years old; an account of what I have been, and something of what I have done, what I have felt, what I have laughed at and what I have cried over – though truthfully I haven't had much cause for weeping.

To write such a record effectively, one has to overcome a great temptation. There's something about the very act of writing that seduces a man into dishonesty, especially when he is writing about himself. In *Eothen,* by A.W. Kinglake, that most delightful of travel books, after some disapproving observations about the numerous saints' days enjoyed by the Smyrniote Greeks, he writes:

"I will let the words stand as a humbling proof that I am subject to that nearly immutable law which compels a man with a pen in his hand to be uttering every now and then some sentiment not his own...I try to set down the thoughts which are fresh within me, and not to pretend any wishes or griefs which I do not really feel; but no sooner do I cease from watchfulness in this regard than my right hand is, as it were, seized by some false angel, and even, you see, I have been forced to put down such words and sentences as I ought to have written, if really and truly I had wished to destroy the saints' days of the beautiful Smyrniotes!....Disturb their saints' days? Oh no!"

Here then is the record. No doubt my right hand has been seized from time to time by some false angel, and I have been persuaded to utter sentiments not truly my own. Probably few of anyone's ideas are without ancestors, whether remembered or forgotten. Or, to put it another way, perhaps the parthenogenetic conception of ideas, like that of babies, is impossible.

CHAPTER ONE

My first eleven years were spent in the United States, where I was born. My father gave us a fine home in those days, always comfortable, strictly but not harshly disciplined, and informed with love and kindness and strong religious conviction of the Methodist persuasion: a pretty good reflection of life as he had learned it and lived it on the old Trueman farm in Point de Bute, N.B. The Truemans have been sitting on that same farm for over two hundred years, and it has been passed down in a direct line from the first owner to son after son – usually the younger son – without exception. My first cousin, Howard, who holds the farm now, will certainly pass it on, he tells me, to one of *his* two sons. Perhaps this reveals something of significance about the breed. Any family that can hold a farm in New Brunswick for two centuries, without once letting it deviate from the direct line of inheritance, and without going broke, must get high marks for stubborn persistence, if for nothing else. I don't believe any of these farmers ever made much money; but they endured, and they gave their families good homes, and their community useful, unselfish service, and leadership, if I read the record right. The first Point de Bute Trueman, William, came to Canada in 1775 from Yorkshire, where things were even tougher than they undoubtedly were in New Brunswick.

My first memories are of Storrs, Connecticut, where father was a member of the faculty of the state Agricultural College from 1907 to 1913. Two memories stand out. He used to get the family together after the evening meal, most often during the winter, seat us around the hearth and read poetry to us. He was wise enough not to fly too high. The one work that I remember very clearly is Scott's *Lady of the Lake* – not the whole thing, but passages that he thought would arouse our interest.

Another memory is of the German Professor. The German Professor was the voice that spoke to us out of the horn on the phonograph which my father bought in pursuance of a new interest. The records were hollow wax cylinders which fitted over the cylinder of the machine. With the phonograph came a series of German lessons. In one of the conversations we followed in the big book, a traveller is asking a policeman how to find the station:

"Bitte, Können Sie mir vielleicht sagen wo der Bahnhof ist?"

The policeman's reply, "Straight on!" had a splendid trilled "r": "Gehen Sie ger-r-r-rade aus!"

It became a household saying. In 1930, in Munich, wanting one day to find a moving-picture theatre, I asked a policeman: "Bitte, Können Sie mir vielleicht sagen wo der Phoebus Palast ist?"

He turned, pointed down the street, and said in the Professor's very voice, "Gehen Sie ger-r-r-rade aus!"

One day, fourteen or fifteen years later, when I was home on vacation, I dodged into the little lavatory on the second floor, off the back hall; there on top of the john was an opened, face-down volume of German poetry with which my father solaced himself when meeting the more demanding calls of nature. What a man!

I remember children I went to school with: Gladys Wheeler, for instance, who lived next door, and who one day was forbidden by her mother to run any more; (I just had wit enough, at eleven years, to figure out that Gladys, early and generously provided with bosom, when she ran made a spectacle, not unnoticed by me, which her mother felt was not nice); the big, burly Costello boys, sons of a local farmer, who bullied the hell out of the rest of us; Azrael Kravitsky, a little Jewish boy who was a wizard with numbers, and left the rest of us far behind when we did what was called "mental arithmetic"; Eliot Savage, an older boy who said dark, not-understood things about the anatomy of girls; Helen Blake, brown-eyed and pretty, with whom I fell desperately in love. And there were the Clinton girls, Ruth, Ruby, and Olive, daughters of one of the professors. The three Trueman boys used to saunter over to the Clinton house from time to time; sometimes invited, sometimes not. Ruby was the leader, the vivacious one, the impudent and provocative one – black-haired and red-lipped. After an hour or so, she would say, "Do you know what I wish?" "No, what?" "I wish I was in my house and you were in yours!"

12

The Trueman boys would take their abrupt departure, not offended, but realizing that the Rubies of this world are without price, and must be dealt with on their own terms, and that the deal is worthwhile. There was Fred Beebe, a brawny, awkward, thick-fingered chap who delivered groceries for his father after school. Beebe had the only store in the community. The sign over the establishment read "General – H.V. Beebe – Merchandise." We called him General Beebe.

In 1912, Thompson, or Tommy as we called him, the brother between Howard and me, died of scarlet fever. All three of us boys came down with it. Our doctor lived in Willimantic, eight miles away. Howard and I tossed off the wretched disease, which was a killer in those days; but Tommy, who was not as robust, was very ill from the start. He was in his thirteenth year when he died.

It was left to Howard to tell me of his death. This he did, quietly and kindly, one night while we were occupying the big double bed in which we had spent the rather easy period of our convalescence. Death I didn't know much about, but I remember well enough my sorrowful and frightened understanding that Tommy was gone, gone for always; that he wouldn't be there any more to play the piano, to show us his drawings, to sit with us at table, and talk, and laugh.

Early in 1913 there appeared at our house a mysterious stranger. He was Dr. Melville Cumming, Principal of the Nova Scotia Agricultural College, which my father had attended for a couple of years before 1895. Dr. Cumming had come to have a look at father and, as it turned out, to offer him the post of Professor of Animal Husbandry and Superintendent of the Experimental Farm. Later that year we set off for Truro, Nova Scotia, or more exactly, for Bible Hill, that curiously named village which was the site of the College and the Farm, and of our family home for the next twenty-four years.

In 1913, after we moved back to Canada, my father began the tiresome process of regaining his Canadian citizenship. I, as a minor, would be granted citizenship when he had received his, and after I had reached the statutory age.

The Bible Hill school, a large wooden building of eight rooms, was situated near the edge of a high steep bank rising from the Salmon River. I don't recall much of what went on in the school-room, but have vivid memories of what went on outside. I was completely unprepared for Bible Hill, a larger community than Storrs, Connecticut, and a much more heterogeneous one. The school-children came from all sorts of families: railroad employees, business men, small tradesmen, mechanics, farm labourers, unskilled day-labourers, college faculty (a few), and the Protestant Orphanage. My first response to Bible Hill was one of embarrassment and confusion. I soon recovered from this cultural shock, and rather easily accommodated myself to a new life-style. All the four-letter words were in general use among the boys. What was to me the dimly imagined mystery of sex was apparently common knowledge here – though I soon found out that was not true. They had the vocabulary, but basically they were as innocent as I was.

In Storrs, I had the advantage – the priceless advantage, as I look back on it – of knowing at first hand the one-room, rural school-house, celebrated in song and legend. I recall a poem which we all learned and chanted together. Only one word of the first stanza escapes me:

Still sits the school-house by the road,
A ragged beggar sunning,
And o'er its (something) ruined walls
The sumach vine is running.

In Bible Hill I had the advantage of a different legendary institution, the "ole swimmin' hole." At the foot of the river-bank a backwater formed a pool; it couldn't have been more than fifteen or twenty feet by eight, and three or four feet at its greatest depth. Down the river-bank we plunged after school, shucking off our clothes and scattering them along the narrow grass verge, and jumped in, shouting, cursing joyously, splashing, horse-playing. This was all new to me. I couldn't swim, for the sufficient reason that I had never before been in swimmin'. I recall that in the early days with this unholy fraternity, I once asked another boy if he planned to "go in bathing" that afternoon. I haven't yet forgotten the jeers provoked by that elegant enquiry.

Sal McLeod, the big muscular son of the village blacksmith, performed a couple of stunts that fascinated me. Sal would throw himself in the water, on his back, let his head and shoulders and legs and feet sink, and yell, at the last moment, when his middle was on high, "Lighthouse Point!" He then performed the complementary exercise: he turned on his belly and just before his bottom was satisfactorily exposed, yelled, "Bare-arse Shoal!" I greatly admired and envied this display of talent. It was a proud day when I found sufficient confidence in myself – and in the water – to do Lighthouse

14

Point and Bare-arse Shoal. Was this an initiation rite? It helped me feel that I was a member of the tribe in good standing.

I did well enough in my studies at the Bible Hill school to be admitted from Grade eight, in 1916, with good credit, to the Colchester County Academy in Truro, which was generally thought, at least by us in Truro, to be the best high school in the Province. The Principal, Dr. D.G. Davis, was I suppose in his late thirties when I first knew him, a determined bachelor, a graduate of Dalhousie and, later of Harvard, with a Ph.D. in Education. An excellent teacher of English language and literature, a firm but fair disciplinarian, he was devoted to the interests of the school and school system – he became the Superintendent for Truro ultimately – and to individual students who needed something more than academic guidance.

Dr. Davis was a sensitive man for whom even the most trifling social *faux pas* was mortifying. I can recall two occasions when I knew him to be so mortified. One of them he told me about, himself, some years after it happened. He had been teaching an English class of boys and girls in Grade eleven, and had assigned them a classroom exercise. "Albert, I told them with the utmost clarity and emphasis that I wanted this little essay written, in 'terth, pissy sentences'." It must have been at least forty-five years later that I told this little story to a university Shakespeare class. A week or so later a charming young woman handed in an essay, and told me: "I've tried my best, Dr. Trueman, to make this 'terth and pissy,' but I'm afraid it's only 'pissy'." O Tempora, O Mores!

"D.G." lived in the boarding-house of Mattie Archibald, a respectable spinster who took in "paying guests." One night about two o'clock, when the house was quiet, "D.G." heard Mattie call out in distress. He jumped out of bed and ran down the hall. She cried out again, and he opened the door to her room. As he stood there, framed in the light from the hallway, he was smashed full in the face with what he afterwards learned was the thunder-jug, as he called it. A strong, tough, and determined man, "D.G." managed to seize the attacker and subdue him, by which time the rest of the house was roused and the police were sent for. The intruder was carted off. When the case was heard in the Town Court House, I got a seat in the gallery. As "D.G." entered and took the witness stand, his face discoloured and swollen, his mouth badly disfigured, the first thing he did was to glance anxiously about the court room. His eyes caught mine, and the colour rose swiftly in his cheeks. Later I

15

understood that to see one of his admiring students in attendance was to him an intolerable situation: to be in court and in that physical condition was bad enough; to be a witness in a case of burglary and violent assault was worse; to have to tell the court how he had been smashed in the face with a thunder-jug, of all weapons, and had been locked in a fight with a black man from the "Island" – the Negro community of Truro – was worst of all.

I owe a great deal to this man. More than any other teacher before I reached university, he gave me some understanding of what scholarship is; of what it means to learn something thoroughly; of how important it is to speak and write well; of the interest and excitement of literature, especially of poetry; and of a couple of basic principles much neglected in our schools today: that no one gets anywhere with his education – or in my opinion with much of anything else – unless he understands the value, as Northrop Frye put it (in "Education and the Rejection of Reality," U. of T. *Graduate*, June 1972), of "repetition in the form of habit and practice," and learns that "freedom emerges and flowers out of discipline."

Another debt I owe to "D.G." is the beginning of a concern for speaking. Friday night was our time – almost our only time – for the school's social life. Usually this took the form of a dance. But "D.G." made us pay for our fun. Before we cleared the floor and got on with the dance he might say, "Now first we'll have a little public speaking from three or four of you. Trueman, in a minute I am going to call on you to get up and talk – not for long, but long enough to put together half a dozen sentences on some piece of current news. Then I'll call on Weir, and then on Florence Smith." It wasn't easy to perform before the other boys and girls – all anxious to get on with the evening's modest revels – and before the teachers, many of whom showed up at these affairs. But these little performances stimulated my interest in speech and in public speaking, and gave me a start on an accomplishment which has been of tremendous value to me all through my professional life.

CHAPTER TWO

Before I go on any further, I want to write something about my father. He was the best man I have ever known. We children called our parents "Father" and "Mother." We were strictly required to do so. There was no sentimental, familiar, disrespectful, and un-Methodist approach to our parents by such foreign, effete, despised names as "pa-pá" and "ma-má," or by "dad," "daddy," "mum," and "mummy." So my father had been brought up, and so were we. It wasn't until after I graduated from Mt. A. that I ever ventured on "Dad," and I don't recall that I did that very often. My mother I never called by any name but "Mother." To be quite honest, she never inspired in me, after I grew up, any wish to break away from the more formal and, as I came to think of it, prim name which had been required of us as children. Here's an odd – and sad – situation.

The unhappy truth is that after I reached the age of, say, sixteen, all my thoughts of home as a place where I wanted to be, or wanted to come back to, for warmth, comfort, understanding, and love – all such thoughts of home were centred entirely on my father.

Earlier memories of Father take me back to Storrs, Connecticut. Many little incidents come to mind. I remember, for instance, being sent from the school-house with a message to my father, who was at the College about a mile away. It was a hot June morning, and I arrived at his office tired and sweaty. What the message was I have no idea; but Father was a school trustee, to whom some cry for help, some request for instruction, might naturally be made. Father took the message without comment, and looked me over. I was glad enough to be free for an hour; but what he saw was a small boy, red-faced, tired, and obviously not looking forward with any pleasure to the long walk back to the school.

As I turned to go he said "Here! Hold on a minute!" He led me outdoors to the primitive bicycle he owned, took the wrench from the little leather bag hanging behind the saddle, lowered the seat to accommodate my short legs and sent me off, with instructions to bring the machine home with me at noon. This was not merely an act of sympathy prompted by my fatigue and my littleness. He knew, and he let me know he knew, by his grin, that I would arrive at the school-house proud to be riding my father's bicycle, and that at noon I would mount in glory, wheel away from my pals, and swiftly leave them all far, far behind. He was like that.

It's a sad thing that all these instances of tenderness and compassionate, imaginative understanding are associated in my memory with my father, rather than with my mother. I recall once being ill, running a little fever and feeling miserable with a sore throat. Father came into my room holding a small bowl of some concoction which he said would soothe my throat and check my cough. "I don't think you're going to like this stuff, but that's no matter. It will be good for you, so take a spoonful." I shut my eyes and opened my mouth. The mixture consisted of honey, with a few drops of lemon juice added. When I opened my eyes Father was looking down at me over his glasses, delighting in my surprise and relief.

Not all my memories of those early days are so pleasant. My father was a strict disciplinarian. The good thing about his discipline was that it was consistent. We knew exactly where we were with him. I recall three principles of conduct which were drilled into us, and which we accepted without dispute or resentment. We had to be courteous to our parents and to all older people – in fact, to everyone. We had to be obedient, to do what we were told promptly and without argument. And we had to be honest – no lying, no pilfering, no sneaking. If we batted a baseball through the living-room window, we were vigorously reminded that we'd been told to play our games at a safe distance from the house; but this kind of minor catastrophe was considered – as the insurance companies put it – an act of God, for which no punishment was in the book. But what Father promised was performed. This certainly was an enormous advantage to us as we tried to make our adjustments to a senior world puzzling to the young. If a child has been allowed to get away with impudence and disobedience twenty times, and on the twenty-first is severely punished, parental indulgence having finally been exhausted, he won't have the vocabulary to say that this is arbitrary, illogical, and unjust.

What he will say is "Not fair!" And he will be right.

As a trustee, Father was naturally concerned about our behaviour in school. He expressed that concern, characteristically, by telling us that any trouble we got into with the teacher would look small in comparison with the trouble that would be waiting for us at home. We understood this point of view perfectly. The world, we well knew, was run by our seniors, and it was not for us to take issue with them, either on general principles, or on specific judgments arising from any troublesome situations we might stir up. As far as school was concerned, it's true that my father's attitude left out of consideration the possibility that we could be unjustly treated by a teacher. But I think that very early we grasped the general notion of "C'est la vie!" "Do as you are told and keep out of trouble" was the rule we observed.

I recall a teacher to whom we children took a dislike, and with the unreflecting cruelty of children, at once made our dislike obvious. At the end of "recess" from 10:15 to 10:30, the teacher rang a large hand-bell, which throughout the day ornamented her desk, to summon us back to our places. By agreement, a few of us one day didn't respond to the bell, but loitered in a group behind the school. That evening my father spoke to me with unusual sternness: "Were you one of the children who didn't return to the school-house after the bell at recess this morning?" I had to say that I was. He took me up to the attic of the newly built house which we had moved into only a few weeks earlier. From my point of view it was much too liberally supplied with laths and other odds and ends of light lumber. He picked up an appropriate instrument and gave me five or six of the best across my stern. The blows were severe enough to sting me into a yelp of discomfort – not really of great pain, because my trousers and underwear gave me good insulation. The point I want to make is that this treatment didn't strike me as at all unfair: I had asked for it, and I got it. In short, my supposed tender little childish soul was not injured. After punishment, all was well – no carry-over of resentment or embarrassment either on my part or on Father's. Needless to say, there were no more revolts against the teacher's authority. Certainly I believe the less corporal punishment the better, and obviously it's not the right punishment for every breach of discipline, or for every child.

Another little episode illustrates another side of my father's nature – his hot temper, which I have inherited. The College boasted a considerable pond, where we loved to skate. Off I went one afternoon with my skates slung over my shoulder, under strict orders to be back home in time for supper, and certainly before it got dark, whichever came earlier. But it was dark, and supper must have been ready for more than half an hour when I belatedly left the pond. Boy-like, I didn't take the road but the pleasanter route down the street, across the lawns, near the houses and in the shadows they cast. As I crossed the last-but-one lawn, I saw my father emerge from our front door and make for the road, buckling the belt of his short mackinaw coat, moving fast and stepping high. I knew where he was bound: I knew it would never do to let him sprint almost a mile to the pond, find that I had left and dash home again, to discover me calmly eating a late supper in the kitchen. So I called out in a faltering voice, "Hello, Father!" I still admire the way in which, having picked up my tentative greeting and spotted me on the lawn, he made a beautiful, wide, sweeping turn to his left, without breaking stride or reducing speed. He came swiftly up behind me and said "Git!" I put for home with Father in hot pursuit. He gave me across the buttocks the flat of his foot, carefully turned sideways, and "heisted" me two or three inches off the ground. Another four steps, and another whomp on my rear, and so it continued. Whomp! Heist! One-two-three-four. Whomp! Heist! until I fled into the house by the back door. When he cooled off – and that didn't take long – he explained that I had not only been disobedient and disturbed the supper arrangements, both serious offences, but had caused him and Mother dreadful imaginings. Had I fallen through the ice? Had no one seen the accident? Was I in fact drowned? In later life I learned that sudden relief from grave anxiety for the safety of one's young often expresses itself in quite irrational anger and violence.

These two incidents, in the attic and on the lawn, are the only ones that I remember in which my father did violence to my person. There may have been one or two others. He had a hot, quick temper, which, with some difficulty, he kept under control. It was often evident that he was indeed controlling it: the face was grim, the craggy jaw was set, the eyes glared, but the temper was held back. I haven't a single recollection arising from these disciplinary occasions that brings sorrow or resentment. On the contrary, they bring respect, laughter, and affection.

Father was a Wesleyan Methodist by upbringing, but that didn't deter him from joining vigorously in the movement for Church

Union with the Presbyterians and the Congregationalists. He was always a loyal churchman, to the best of my recollection, and was always the superintendent of the Sunday school wherever we went. All through my days in Truro, 1913-1924, Sunday was a tough ordeal. Before church in the morning it was my chore to go down to the Experimental Farm barns and harness the little hackney that Father drove, hitch the horse to the surrey – no fringe on top, but of that vehicular family – and drive back to the house, where Father took over. Four of us piled into the surrey – Howard walked – and set off for the Pleasant Street Methodist Church; in later years to the St. Andrew's United Church, formerly Presbyterian. We got back home at 12:30 or thereabouts, had Sunday dinner, and pushed off again about 2:30 for Sunday school. Back we came at about 4:30 or 4:45, in time to have a light Sunday supper, after which we again set out, at 6:30, for evening service. When I reached the age of sixteen, or thereabouts, I was given freedom on Sunday evenings to attend the church of my choice. That was usually the First Presbyterian Church on Prince Street, because it had the best music. It was clearly understood, of course, that I would go to church somewhere.

Sunday school was for me a curious fusion of pleasure and boredom. Playing the hymns on my violin was a pleasure. Rosalie Smith, an excellent musician, played the piano, and Frank Dickie, a Bible Hill pal of no fixed church connection, came along, "just for the hell of it," as he said, to play the cornet. He was very good at it indeed, and could do something which I believe he called triple-tonguing. I committed many offences against music on those Sunday afternoons. Frank played the melody, and I elected to provide an obligato. I rejoiced to take the tenor part as written in the hymn book, transpose it to the treble clef, and render it – that's a good word – an octave higher than the original. Father didn't care much for my peculiar performance, and small blame to him, but this remarkable feat of musicianship gained me great credit and even local fame among Truro's young. In moments of unusual ecstasy I would depart from the hymn book entirely, and soar away, improvising a part all my own. I must admit that Father's taste in hymns was not good. For Sunday school he preferred "rousers": sprightly, fast-moving tunes that tended to dispel the gloom that I'm sure he felt was the enemy of religion, particularly of religion for the young. He avoided the more lugubrious and saccharine words and melodies of such deplorable compositions as "I walked in the garden alone," "The old rugged cross," and "The ninety-and-nine," although he countenanced, "Shall we gather at the river?" It had marked rhythm and better pace.

The boredom began when I and half a dozen other boys retreated to the small, unattractive cell in which A.R. Coffin dispensed scriptural knowledge and morality, as the current Sunday school lesson dictated. "A.R." was the owner and publisher of the *Truro Daily News*. I had no objection to either scriptural knowledge or morality; but A.R. Coffin, short, portly, and unbelievably dull in his delivery of the divine message, was pretty hard to take. I can see and hear him yet, sitting on a kitchen chair, twiddling the watch-chain draped over his belly, and droning away about the missionary journeys of St. Paul. Apart from the music, my principal memories of Sunday school are of boredom and dejection.

Much as I loved and admired my father when I was a child, I was never wholly at ease with him until I was rather more than halfway through my teens. Always a father figure, at the same time he was a discipline and duty figure: I regarded him with some awe and, on occasion, with a touch of fear. No other response was possible to a man of such strength, of such monumental integrity, of such dominant personality, despite the sympathy and the tenderness of which so often he was capable.

Then, of course, there was the much-talked of generation gap. He was an agriculturist, a descendant of the farm, and a churchman. When I became old enough to notice such things, I didn't like his clothes, which he got from an immigrant English tailor who belonged to our church. They didn't seem quite right, not like the clothes worn by the successful business men of the town. Father's were made of excellent cloth, meticulously put together, lined and sewn with great care, but the cut, the style, was provincial, farmerish, emphatically "not with it": the jacket was much too long and unshaped; the bulky trousers drooped too low over the shoes. He didn't play golf or belong to the tennis club. Our church was unfashionable. These matters disturbed me, and made me slightly uneasy with him on public occasions. He embarrassed me whenever we drove along Prince Street in the carriage furnished by the College, behind Fred, the little hackney. Father sat in a characteristic pose: leaning slightly forward, he put his left hand on his left leg, just above the knee, with the elbow extended to his left; he put his right elbow on his right leg, just above the knee, with his fore-arm nearly erect, and gathered the reins in his fingers. More often than not, as we

22

tooled along the street, he hummed or even sang the words of some gospel hymn which we had used that week in Sunday school. I tried to make myself small and keep out of sight and sound of the passers-by. Eventually I got over this embarrassment and began to join in, contributing an improvised bass to the tune of the day, and not caring a damn if anyone thought us quaint or peculiar. But that emancipation from youthful self-consciousness didn't take place until I was seventeen or eighteen.

Mark Twain tells of a similar relationship with his father. If my memory is correct he tells of going through somewhat the same stages as I've been recalling, and suddenly at age twenty-one or twenty-two wondering how the old man had managed to learn so much in the last two or three years. The embarrassment that left me in my mid-teens was succeeded by ease and pleasure in his company, even though his tailor was still clumsy and old-fashioned, and Father made no attempt to cut a figure in the so-called high society of the town, in which I rather fancied I was beginning to get a footing. At the age of twenty-one or twenty-two, I began to understand and value and respond profoundly to his humanity, his humour, his sanity, his tolerance, his wisdom, his love.

This happy relationship lasted, unshaken, until his death. The last few months of 1936 and the January of 1937 were heart-breaking. He was suffering from cancer of the prostate gland, and had twice gone to Montreal for operations. It was of no use; the cancer could not be checked. Once, near the end, he asked me to write to his surgeon in Montreal, Dr. MacKenzie, to ask if there was anything more to be done. I wrote, and got a sympathetic, kindly letter in return that told me there was no hope. I had to make that report to Father. A day or so later, as I stood beside his bed, he looked up at me and, using the nickname the family had adopted, said, "I'm right up against it, Bill." Those were the last words I ever heard him speak. Not long afterwards I stood again by his bed watching him as he lay in a coma, and counting the pulsations of the artery in his poor, gaunt throat. They stopped. He was gone.

His memory is still bright with me. I come across something in my reading that he would have liked; I hear a funny story that I should like to have told him; I catch myself using a gesture or falling into a posture that reminds me that I am indeed his son.

CHAPTER THREE

By the time I was ready for College, I had no money, and my father had none. I went to work for Avery Hiltz in his men's clothing store on Prince Street. Atbout this time I discovered that I had a voice, and began to sing in the church choir. I got a part in a local production of *Pinafore* in which I remember I was to sing, "He is an Englishman! and it's greatly to his credit...." On the day before the performance I was rushed to the hospital with a bad appendix, which was safely carved out of me while my pals, at a last rehearsal, were bracing themselves for the show. Once out of hospital I decided not to go back to my job in the store. Someone suggested that I register at the Provincial Normal College, for the brief teacher-training course that was just about to open. This was known as the MPQ course; it lasted for three or four months. The initials stood for "Minimum Professional Qualification." I doubt if the course could properly be called "professional" but it was certainly "minimum." (For the credit of Nova Scotia I must report that the course was abandoned long ago.) After I had passed the course, in which happily there were no examinations, a miracle happened. "D.G.," who had been made Superintendent of the Truro School System, offered me a job in the new Alice Street School, teaching Grades four and five.

As I look back to the appointment I wonder how "D.G." could have had enough faith in me, and the unqualified gall, to make it. With the exception of one hour, in which I had told a story to some very young children in the Willow Street School – this was called practice teaching – I had never stood before a class. Now I had to find ways to keep order, to teach youngsters of nine and ten years to spell, read, and write and – I recall this particularly – to understand and begin to do fractions. But wonderfully, I had few difficulties and enjoyed myself tremendously. As a matter of fact I have relished teaching more than anything else I have ever done. I have had a number of different and exciting admistrative jobs, but the truth is that teaching has given me my greatest professional satisfaction, and the titles which I have been proudest to bear are "teacher" and "professor."

It proved not at all difficult to get my two classes under control and on my side. Children of this age, once persuaded that you are "for" them and "with" them, give you an almost embarrassing measure of trust and devotion. I recall parents who good-humouredly complained to me that suggestions and advice and even orders given at home were often countered with, "But Mr. Trueman says to do it *this* way." Marvellous! But they soon grow out of this delightful and innocent state of faith and trust, and then the teacher has to be more skilful and a little tougher.

After Christmas of my first year at the new Alice Street School, Grade six was added to the curriculum and I was "promoted" to be its teacher. This gave me, as I recall it, the wholly unofficial title of School Principal. One of the dodges I used in order to get the class on my side was to reward the kids for a pretty well-behaved week by bringing my violin to the school on Friday afternoons.

Back in the Storrs, Connecticut period, my father, on a whim had once decided to make me a violin. He appropriated a cedar cigar-box belonging to my mother's father and turned it into a crude fiddle – actually not so crude. He sandpapered the thing, polished it up, cut f-holes in it, and attached a neck fashioned from a stick of maple, carved a nice scroll, fitted in pegs, and strung it up. He even managed to insert a sound-post inside the belly of this remarkable instrument. "When you can play "Yankee Doodle" on this contraption I'll buy you a real violin," he told me.

The fiddle, though its tone must have been hellish, was playable, and with some tuition from my father, who had done a little country fiddling in his day, I was soon able to scrape out "Yankee Doodle," and Father bought me a god-awful factory-made violin for something like six dollars. Now I was properly launched on my musical career.

When we moved to Canada in 1913 I continued the violin lessons I had begun in Storrs. I had to have a better fiddle, and I bought one for fifteen dollars, which I earned by working at various odd jobs. It was a curious instrument, reputedly Russian in origin, or in design, with the edges of the belly rounded instead of sharply defined. It had a small but sweet tone, and became a precious possession. I made good progress and loved my teacher almost as much as I did my new violin. To tell the truth, she aroused me physically. I was now about fourteen, and getting more and more curious about more and more things. A violin lesson was for me something more than an hour of musical tuition. But I was still a kid, and much as I adored Mrs. G. I skipped my lesson one day; the lure of the "ole swimmin' hole" was too much for me. After a wonderful hour with the gang down at the foot of the river bank, I pulled my fiddle case out of the bush where I had hidden it, dried my hair, and lit out for home, hoping my father wouldn't suspect that I had skipped my lesson. But of course Mrs. G. had telephoned to ask what had happened to Albert, and my father soon got the truth out of me.

The Boston Symphony Orchestra, or a segment thereof, was giving a concert that evening in the Princess Theatre, and my father had promised to take me. He made the point that a young man – so he called me – who wasn't interested enough in music to take his violin lesson would scarcely care to hear the Boston Symphony Orchestra. But strict disciplinarian though he was, he was a very wise and kindly man, and he saw at once that the punishment he hinted at would be out of proportion to my not very outrageous crime; missing that concert would indeed have been a cruel deprivation to a boy who had already made it clear that he had a genuine love of music. We went to the concert. I skipped no more lessons.

Now on Friday afternoons – we're back in Grade six, at the Alice Street School – I made it a practice to knock off work early, and read my class stories and poems, and play on my violin. This Friday afternoon program became famous throughout the school, and I was entreated to leave my door open so that the fiddle performances could be heard in other classrooms, where doors were also left open. I recall that on invitation I moved about to other grades so that those who had no fiddler on hand could get the music straight from the horse's mouth, as it were.

I was not an accomplished player. I played simple things, tunes and songs the youngsters knew, and such easy compositions as Schumann's *Träumerei*, somebody's *Chanson Triste*, an arrangement of something from *Cavalleria Rusticana*, the *Minuet in G*, Handel's *Largo*, and even jigs like *The Irish Washerwoman* and the *Arkansas Traveller*. You can imagine how satisfying and ego-inflating this was for me, and, I'm sure, how welcome and even exciting it was for the children.

At sixteen years of age I was nearly full-grown, a pretty muscular and fairly athletic young man. What to do with the summer vacation? My father believed, I'm sure, in what is often called "the Protestant work ethic." Accordingly, he put me to work on the Agricultural College Experimental Farm. A number of boys, and a few young men home from college, were taken on for the summer months as extra help for hoeing vast fields of turnips and mangolds, for haying, and other seasonal chores. At first he hesitated to give me a job, I suppose because he didn't want to be accused of nepotism. He talked with me very frankly and sternly before I began my first summer's work, pointing out that I was the boss's son, and that shirking or cheating on my part would be conspicuous and talked about, and a discredit not only to me but to him; in short, if he gave me a job, I would have to work hard and earn my wages. I must say that I heeded his warning, and toiled honestly enough.

In my bracket the wages were ten cents an hour for a ten-hour day. I worked from seven in the morning to noon, and from one to six p.m., and even to eight or nine o'clock in good haying weather, with no extra pay for overtime. Believe me, I have never since worked so hard to earn a dollar.

The work was monotonous and tiring. Working in the barn with the animals, particularly the horses, was more interesting, but a poor trade-off for fresh air and sunshine. The younger chaps were thrown in with the older day-labourers, a good-natured lot, expert at doing the minimum required to pass the foreman's inspection. Much of their language was a fluent, adult version of the profanities and obscenities to which I'd become accustomed at Bible Hill School. I toughed this out for a couple of summers. Then one June day my father said to me, "How would you like a different job this summer? The Horticultural Department wants some help in the greenhouses and gardens. You'd be doing various chores, giving a hand with bedding-out plants, cleaning up the tools at the end of the day." I jumped at the chance of a more "refined" job, not so heavy and tiring, and on the whole likely to be more interesting.

One morning the Head Gardener needed a cart-load of manure. I was told to give a hand to George Madill, the teamster who was to fetch it. For reasons that I couldn't imagine, the manure at the

College Farm – and God knows there was enough of it – was not the right kind. As I said to George, "I don't see why we have to go to Newt Lee's Livery Stable for this stuff. After all, shit is shit!" George agreed with me, but knew no more about the matter than I did.

Off we set, rumbling along the streets of Truro to Newt Lee's establishment on the Esplanade, just about opposite the CNR station. We backed the huge cart into a narrow alley, and parked it under a small window that must have been six or seven feet from the ground. When we entered the stables, Newt led us to a dark, filthy hole which was the repository of this special, life-giving fertilizer. It was a smallish room, some feet deep in manure. We forked the manure out the little window into the cart below. Since the window was shoulder high, and kept getting even higher as we lowered the level, fragments of the abominable stuff fell back off the fork on to my neck and shoulders and hands. After the foul job was done, George threw a tarpaulin over the load and lashed it down. I was tempted to tell him that I wanted to stretch my legs and would walk back to the farm, over a mile away. But something, I don't know what, pride perhaps, or shame, made me abandon this unworthy ploy, and so, mounted on this huge load of shit *de luxe*, we moved slowly and majestically along Walker Street to the Salmon River bridge, I fervently hoping that we wouldn't be seen by my current girl-friend, whose house we had to pass *en route*. I thought that this chore by no means answered the job-description my father had given me.

These days on the farm provided formative experiences. When I was perhaps seventeen, my father asked if I had any idea what I wanted to do with my life. Farm boy though he had been, and professional agriculturalist though he was, he shook with laughter when I replied, "I don't know yet what I want to do; but one thing I'm sure of: it will be something out of sight and sound and, may I add, smell, of a farm."

Another experience of those days edged me in the direction I was already taking. For several years the Truro YMCA had sponsored a winter series of lectures, given by very able men, most of whom were brought in from Halifax. My father once said to me, "Never lose the chance to hear a famous man or an expert. Now and then you'll be disappointed, but seven or eight times out of ten you'll be richly paid for your trouble." Accordingly, we went together to these Sunday afternoon lectures. I remember hearing Henry Munro, Dalhousie historian, later Chief Superintendent of Education for the Province;

Dawson, Dalhousie physicist; Archie MacMechan, critic, author, and head of the Dalhousie Department of English; Clarence McKinnon, theologian, Principal of Pine Hill Divinity College and silver-tongued orator; Ralph Connor, the novelist; and my Uncle George, President of Mount Allison University. I can't honestly say that I remember a single thing these men said. But I *do* remember the profound impression they made on me. I wanted to be able to talk like that, to have that kind of bearing and authority; to have such mastery of a subject that I would be called from far away to address an interested and respectful audience.

When I look back over all this – debating in High School, public speaking at our High School Friday evening social affairs, attending the Truro YMCA Sunday afternoon lectures with my father, and debating at Mount Allison – I realize that very early and progressively I was committed to the serious public use of the spoken word; in fact, one of the colours in the pattern of my life was selected in my youthful days; it has never faded out, no matter where I have been or what I have been doing.

CHAPTER FOUR

After two years at the Alice Street School, Dr. Davis brought me into the High School – the Colchester County Academy. I was even more astonished by this decision than I was by his having given me a job in the lower school. I spent a year at the Academy, teaching algebra, English and history. Associating with the other teachers, all older than myself and academically more advanced, was pleasanter than I had dared hope. I particularly remember the kindness of Jack Smith, a graduate of Mt. Allison. Jack was handsome, athletic – he had been a hockey star at university – modest and friendly. He might easily have taken a lofty attitude toward me, with my Grade XII certificate so dubiously acquired. Instead, he accorded me equal status and was always cordial, thoughtful, and helpful.

In 1924, at the age of twenty-two (three or four years later than most of my contemporaries), I entered the "Freshie-Soph" year at Mount Allison. My financial position was shaky. While I was teaching in Truro my father had said "You'll want to go to university pretty soon. I'm somewhat in debt," (a chronic condition with him for at least forty years) "and I can't help you now. I propose that while you're teaching, you turn over to me as much of your salary as you can spare, and when the time comes for you to go to Mt. A., I'll see you through, or at least as nearly through as I can manage." This arrangement seemed sensible to me, and I accepted it. Father was able to see me through two of my three years. In my last year I borrowed a few hundred dollars from the Royal Bank on a note endorsed by him. It took all of my first year after graduation to pay it off.

My days at Mount Allison were very good days indeed. Having taught school for three years and having worked in summer vacations on the Experimental Farm, I'd had some of the nonsense knocked out of me. I lack, in some degree, the methodistic, somewhat puritanical strain so strong in the Trueman tribe. It's a matter of common observation that the force of senior example is frequently weak in families. My Trueman grandfather did not smoke or drink. My father did not smoke or drink. My Uncle George, and my Uncle Will, who held the old home farm, did not smoke or drink. My cousin, who holds the farm today, does not smoke or drink. My older brother Howard smokes almost not at all, and does not drink. But I, after I had reached my late twenties, took to both these delightful indulgences like a duck to water.

My drinking days began rather late. I didn't get to Mount Allison until I was twenty-two, and up to that time I hadn't tasted alcohol. All through my undergraduate days I didn't drink, partly because of my good Methodist background, partly because I had no particular urge to drink, partly because the President of this small but delightful university was my Uncle George, an austere man, at least as far as smoking and drinking were concerned, and I didn't want to let him down. Furthermore, in those days, 1924-1927, students who used "intoxicating beverages" were liable to expulsion.

When I went to Oxford in 1928, at the advanced age of twenty-six, I quickly discovered that everyone to whom I had to look for every kind of guidance, drank. My fellow undergraduates – most of them – drank. Not only were there no regulations forbidding drinking, but the College would sell me beer and wine on credit; townspeople who gave me delightful hospitality, drank, and would serve me liquor. Under these circumstances, there's nothing for a chap to do but alter his convictions.

I recall that my tutor, Nevill Coghill, a delightful man, hurried into one of my first tutorials rather late, having been delayed by one of the infrequent lectures he gave, full of apologies and exclaiming, "My God, I'm dry. Would you care to join me, Trueman, in a glass of sherry?" At that time, not having sorted out the rationale of drinking, I said politely and no doubt stiffly, "No thank you, Sir." But I soon came to the conclusion that there must be something wrong with the forbidding attitudes on which I had been brought up.

My interest in English Literature, stimulated in the first place by the example of my father and my brother Howard, and in the second place by Dr. D.G. Davis at the Colchester County Academy, continued without slackening. Mount Allison's one-man English department was Professor Morley Tweedie, who had been there for half a century – more than that, counting his undergraduate days. During his five or six years of post-graduate study abroad, as a Gilchrist Scholar to begin with, he studied at London, Göttingen, Berlin, and Edinburgh. His presentation of literature was scholarly, organized, lucid and, on the whole, unemotional. For some students he was too dry. For me he was just right. I very much needed the discipline of thorough and exact study, and exposure to a clear, logical, and "dry" mind; the emotions I could supply for myself, without professorial stimulus. At his lectures I took careful and copious notes. When I went to Oxford I took them with me, and found them extremely useful. In those days at Oxford, lectures were not greatly valued; and I'm bound to say that most of the lecturers I heard made it only too clear why this judgment prevailed.

Two other professors at Mt. A. made a special impression on me. One was John Line, a young theologian from England, a man of brilliant mind and a delightful sense of humour. He gave the course in Religious Knowledge, which, I believe, was compulsory for all undergraduates. On reflection, I'm not sure that it was required of everyone – perhaps only of Arts students; but then, I ask myself, by what kind of logic could the Engineers have been excused, who, it always seemed to me, stood in special need of any grace that might be picked up from such a course of instruction? By definition, this was a course which very few undergraduates wanted to take and most of them dreaded. But under Dr. Line it was a pleasurable and stimulating experience. Rather than making a compulsory pass exercise difficult, he made it interesting.

I am also grateful to him for the coaching he gave to the debating squad, of which I was made the leader in my first year because the man first chosen fell ill and could not act. There was one big Maritime inter-collegiate debate each year, and in the successive springs of 1925, 1926, and 1927, we won the argument with Dalhousie, St. Francis Xavier, and Acadia. But I was never completely happy with the system of preparation we used. Debating was then taken very seriously by the faculty and by many of the students, who got their practice and a good deal of entertainment in the Eurhetorian Society – now, I learn, defunct. When we began to prepare for these inter-collegiate debates we met with a faculty advisory committee consisting, in my day, of John Line, Morley Tweedie, Norman Guy (Newfoundland economist and Harvard man), and Roy Liddy (philosopher and psychologist). We prepared our line of argument, had it considered and improved by our advisors, and then retreated to write out our speeches. We then memorized them, pretty well word for word, and took them back to the committee, where we recited them, parrot fashion. We had three or four, or even five, meetings of this kind, in which our language was checked, our manner of speaking and our platform deportment were criticized, and our arguments were again examined and even altered, if the committee thought it necessary. On one occasion I ventured a mild protest, when I judged that what I was saying and how I was saying it had become too little "Trueman" and too much "committee." I was shot down at once.

Another professor who made a lasting impression on me was Dr. J.W. Cohoon, a fine classics scholar, Canadian, and a graduate of Princeton. Jimmy Willy, as we all called him, in affection, was one of the shyest men I ever knew. When you met him in the street he kept his eyes straight ahead until he was sure you had uttered a word or made some gesture of recognition; then he hastily and nervously acknowledged your greeting, in fact, almost over-acknowledged it. Like most of the professors at Mt. A. at the time, he carried a preposterous lecture load – eighteen or twenty hours a week, teaching all the Latin and Greek, and all the German, at which he was excellent, although German was a side-line for him.

I never became much of a Latin scholar, but I learned much from Jimmy Willy. The example of fine scholarship was important to me then, and has remained important to me ever since. But he stood for other values than pure scholarship. He was a gentleman in the finest sense of that ambiguous word, courteous and considerate to all of us, generous to our needs, and gentle in his bearing. When I came back from Oxford to be Tweedie's Assistant Professor, only three years after I had taken my last lecture from Jimmy Willy, he said to me one day, in his soft voice and shy manner, "Professor Trueman, I *do* wish I had your great knowledge of English Literature." From anyone else I should have strongly suspected irony, but not from him. I was bowled over by the remark; knowing that as a scholar I could never aspire to be in his company, I realized that this was his gentle and generous way of welcoming a very green young man into the academic fraternity of the learned.

We were fortunate in those years to have men of this calibre on the faculty of our small University – in my time, both as an undergraduate and professor, I don't believe that total registration was ever much more than six hundred. I have not named all the distinguished men on the campus. There was Sidney Hunton, the mathematician, another Gilchrist Scholar and graduate of the University of London. He served Mt. A. brilliantly for a year or two more than half a century. I never took mathematics from him, but when I came back from Oxford, I cultivated his friendship. I found out that he had two much-loved diversions: he read Trollope, and he read the Greek classics. I don't mean that he studied Greek; he read Greek for pleasure. He must have come close to answering the description of a scholar who could read Plato "with his feet on the fender." It would be difficult to imagine a man who, in the course of half a century of professional life, had lived more usefully for others and more richly for himself.

Dr. Harold ("Strut") Bigelow, the chemist, was a man of significant influence on the campus, in the class-room and laboratory and in the men's residence, of which he was the "Dean." The scholarship of Tweedie and Hunton, which was basically sound, must have suffered during the half-century that each of them spent at Mt. A. They carried such huge loads of teaching responsibility, in addition to all the other duties they assumed in the running of the place, that I can't believe either of them had time for anything that could be fairly called research. Tweedie succeeded in getting away for a year at Harvard. He was Dean of the men's residence at that time; just before he returned, the building was burned to the ground with all his possessions but one cup and saucer. "I felt," he said, "like a man without a past." Perhaps the most significant thing I can say about Tweedie, Line, Cohoon, Guy, Hunton, Bigelow, Roy Fraser, and Liddy – and others – is that they commanded the complete respect of all serious students, for their knowledge, for their character, for their bearing and appearance, and for their devotion to the University and to our personal needs.

I must say the same of my Uncle George, the President. He was a man of rather stern aspect, with a battle-ship jaw and an erect and stiff way of carrying himself and walking, but no one had more sympathy for the erring student – the student who got drunk and disorderly, the student who was convicted of pilfering in the residence, the student who made a co-ed pregnant, the co-ed who became pregnant, the student who was doing little or no work. With all of them he reasoned, persuaded – and forgave. A prominent

Churchman, deeply religious, who governed his personal life and his official life by the tenets of The New Testament, he made no bones about quoting the Gospels when pressed for a justification of his attitudes and policies. Inevitably, since his signature was George J. Trueman, he was sometimes called, by the flippant and unregenerate, "George Jesus." I don't believe he ever knew that.

I worked hard at my studies, although I took a full part in the social life of the University and in various club activities. I didn't take any serious part in sports. I turned out one Fall for English Rugby, but wasn't much good at it. I played tennis for the University; in fact, I was captain of the team one year. I put the shot in a track and field meet with UNB, and defeated my only opponent, Bev Macaulay, whom, many years later, I brought to UNB as the Business Manager; and I ran a lap in the 4 x 1/4 mile relay against Acadia, which we won. I was given the Alumni Honours Prize on graduation day. This was awarded to the student, who, entering as a Freshie-Soph in the second year, had the highest average throughout his stay at the University. But I missed getting my Honours Certificate because I failed to make the Honours standard in Old English, much to my shame and to Professor Tweedie's sorrow. I have no excuses to make for this disgrace, for disgrace it was. The truth is that I wasn't interested in the subject, and didn't work at it. It wasn't until years later that I responded to the value and the attraction of the ancient literature of our language. At Oxford I made some improvement, but much of what I know about Old English and Linguistics I acquired after I'd finished my university course. Since I had to teach the subject at Mt. A. after Professor Tweedie retired, I had to get on with it then.

During my first year at Mt. A. I met a young man who became my close friend, and is now, with the exception of Jack Smith, my oldest friend in all the world. This was Fred Johns, now Air Vice Marshal C.F. Johns (ret.). Fred came up to Mt. A. from Bermuda, where his father had a senior civilian post at Ireland Island, the British naval base. We were drawn together by many common interests, the chief of which was no doubt music. Freddie had an excellent bass voice which led him to join, as I did, both church and University choirs. In our second year we decided to unite in a scheme of civilized living that worked out beautifully. Residence rooms were drawn by lot in the Spring, in anticipation of Fall occupancy. Between us we got an excellent single room at the front of the huge building on the third floor, and a not-so-good single at the back, which we shared as a bedroom, making the front room into a study. If one of us wanted to read far into the night and the other wanted to sleep, there were no difficulties. Furthermore, getting the beds and bureaus out of the living-room created an atmosphere which, though scarcely home-like, was conducive to study, and, of course, to much easy conversation, story-telling, and laughter, all of which we enjoyed and came to value highly.

One of the very good things in a very lucky life has been this enduring friendship; friendship which, following Dr. Johnson's advice to Sir Joshua Reynolds, we have kept "in constant repair." In a letter to Sir Joshua, written in 1784, Johnson wrote – and I echo the sentiment as I think of C.F. Johns – "…we are now old acquaintance, and perhaps few people have lived so much and so long together, with less cause of complaint on either side."

CHAPTER FIVE

I graduated from Mt. A. in 1927, not knowing what I was going to do in the immediate future. I wanted to continue my studies, and I wanted to teach in a university, but I had no money at all, and my father had none to spare. Just as the year ended, the Principal of Stanstead College, P.Q., came on the scene, looking for staff. He took three of us – Helen Duchemin, Douglas Lawley, and me.

Stanstead was a private, co-educational, preparatory, boarding school. I spent a year there, as the Headmaster of the Academic Department. Whatever else I learned in that brief experience, I learned this: private, co-educational, preparatory boarding schools are the devil to manage. I don't suggest they shouldn't exist. But when you tot up all the problems that arise in running either a girls' school or a boys' school, and then add to them the special and vexing and nearly insoluble problems created by housing the sexes together, in one residential building, you are asking for more, much more, than the usual difficulties which characterize, God knows, any effort to educate and discipline the young.

The Reverend Mr. MacKenzie, the Principal, was a good man, concerned for the welfare of the students, gentle and kind, but weak on the discipline which the school needed. One day as he was crossing the grounds from his house to the main building, he heard a boy singing a bawdy song. The lad was in the shower-room on the third floor, near an open window. The Principal, to my astonishment, brought the matter up next morning at assembly. He was clearly horrified: his voice trembled and his face was flushed. Unfortunately, since he couldn't very well bring himself to quote the words of the song, only a few of us had any idea what the fuss was all about. Now, if you grant that something needed to be done about this incident – and

37

I, for one, thought very little needed to be done – the Principal's tactics were hopelessly wrong. If he had consulted me, which I'm sure he didn't dream of doing, I could have suggested that he first identify the culprit – not too difficult a thing to do. He should then have called the boy into his private office and explained that he was not shocked by the song, that he was quite aware that normal boys talked – and sang – in this ribald vein on occasion. He should then have said: "If you *must* do this sort of thing, for Heaven's sake don't do it in front of an open window."

Before I ever reached Stanstead I realized that I would begin my work there under a handicap: many years earlier, Uncle George had been the Principal of the School. I knew that he had been held in respect and affection by students and staff alike, and I soon found out that his name was still remembered and greatly honoured. But, alas, I was no "Uncle George." My conception of duties and responsibilities was much too narrow. I think that even then I was a pretty good teacher; certainly I had no particular difficulty in creating interest in my literature courses, and in keeping discipline in the classroom. But what I hadn't reckoned on was that at the Stanstead of 1927-28 – I think I'm correct in saying this – the students were divided into two main groups (no doubt that's an over-simplification, but 'twill serve): the well-behaved boys and girls who were having difficulty with their academic work; and the boys and girls, many of them quite able and usually from the larger centres, who were out of control, both at home and at school, and were getting into trouble with authority. Both of these groups had been sent to Stanstead in the parental hope that they would be given the kind of concerned, individual attention they needed for their studies, and, for many of them, the kind of firm, sustained discipline, involving regular hours and compulsory study periods, that had not been brought to bear on them at home or in school.

This state of affairs flabbergasted me. I didn't know what to make of it, or what to do about it. At that time, I felt that when I had conscientiously done my teaching, cleaned up the modest administrative duties that were laid on the Headmaster of the Academic Department, and taken a modest part in the social life of the place, I had discharged my obligations to school and students. It soon became evident that this was not good enough. It wasn't in the tradition of Uncle George, or indeed of the school, and it didn't comply with

Principal MacKenzie's motivations, unselfish, honourable, and helpful as they were.

One day, early in February, or it may have been late in January, there arrived at the school a tall, beetle-browed young man, with sullen resentment and insubordination written across his face. I don't recall his name, where he came from, or why he had turned up at this very odd and inconvenient time. I talked with him, and pretty quickly took his measure as a hopeless student and a determined rebel. In the interests of the young man's general welfare and academic prospects, the Principal called me into his office to discuss a program into which he might be inserted. The Principal talked about arranging a special course of study, after it had been ascertained what the young man knew – ("If anything," I muttered under my breath); he talked about special tuition from me and from other teachers; about letting him sit in the regular classes, in the hope that he might pick up something, and leaving him unbothered by normal requirements, and questions that he couldn't answer. To all this I made an impatient response, expressing, I'm afraid, my complete indifference to the fellow and my intention to ignore him. MacKenzie's face flushed in annoyance as he expressed his disappointment in me. He had earlier suggested that I might be considered as his successor; now he withdrew that suggestion and reproved me for not taking a greater interest in the students outside the classroom – their personalities, their morals, their pastimes, their problems of social adjustment.

The young man in question, I may say, behaved exactly as I had thought he would. He hadn't been at the school for forty-eight hours before he was bucking our pretty reasonable rules of conduct, and he did no study whatsoever. But that, of course, is not the point. I should have had a crack at doing something for him, even though I was convinced that certain failure stared me in the face. But I remember that I justified myself by such immature and no doubt selfish reflections as, "When I came here I had no idea that I was supposed to be joining the staff of a reform school," and "I don't conceive my role to be that of a Sunday-school teacher." (To tell the truth, in my subsequent teaching I have never completely succeeded in banishing these convictions and resentments, although I have greatly modified them.) I don't mean to suggest that this year was for me a hopeless personal failure or that I was a dead loss to the school and to its students. Some of the teachers and some of the students will have remembered me, I'm sure, as having been pleasant and helpful.

There was a colleague at Stanstead whose friendship I enjoyed and with whom I talked over my problems and gossiped about the school, and many other matters. This was Harlow Martin, the head of the Conservatory of Music. He had been blind since infancy. He told me that with the exception of one or two colours, red being one of them, he had no visual memories whatever. He didn't know, couldn't "see" in his mind's eye, what a tree looked like, a flower, a human face. I found it impossible to imagine what it must have been to live for decades – he was in his forties or early fifties then – in complete dependence upon four senses only. Obviously the sense of touch was of the utmost importance to him. Indeed, as Aristotle pointed out, without the sense of touch, organic life would be impossible. Harlow was a man of great sensitivities, especially to the people about him, and he was very brave. I remember driving him from Stanstead to a neighbouring town in Vermont on a winter day when the highway was treacherous. Once I put on the brake a little too heavily and the car went instantly into a wide, sickening skid that turned us completely around. "Going back to Stanstead, Albert?" said Harlow in a gentle voice, quite unperturbed, not gripping the side of the car, not pushing down the floor-boards. I admired that self-possession, that courage in the blind man who sat there beside me, wholly in my hands, in the black dark that gave him no points of reference, having nothing but his keen sense of movement and change in its direction to inform him of what was going on. I myself was considerably scared for a panic moment or two. But not, apparently, Harlow.

In March, the school gave a set of mid-term tests to everyone, in all grades. I had found out by Christmas that many of our students didn't bother to show up for their examinations. For this coming set in March I tried to make sure that all my students would be in attendance. The captain of the football team, a clever enough lad, had been ill during the Christmas recess and didn't get back into classes for over a month after term began. He asked to be excused from writing. I explained to him courteously and carefully that I wanted everyone on hand. I acknowledged he was at a disadvantage, but I assured him that I was confident he could do better than he expected, and I argued that writing the paper would be good practice for him. In any event, I told him, "If you don't do well, I shan't hold your low marks against you at the end of the year." He turned away in anger, and rudely. He showed up at the examination, and after half an hour, swaggered noisily up to my desk, threw his paper down contemptuously, without a word on it but his name, and sloped out of the room.

After the examination was closed I went out to the business office of the school for something, I don't know what, and there was my young friend, asking for the key to the gymnasium, which was closed for the examination period. The office was strictly out of bounds to students. I went up to him. "Tom," I said, (that wasn't his name) "I've had about enough. You're out of bounds here, and you have no business trying to get into the gym. I suggest you go up to your room and do a little work." He then did a beautiful piece of acting: he ran his eye up and down my person with what I can only call sneering contempt. "Dumb insolence" I believe is the army term. It was well done; too well done! I boiled. I took him by the arm to show him to the door. He threw off my arm violently and raised his fist as if to let me have one. I beat him to the punch, however, and let *him* have one, which knocked him to the floor. (The punch was sheer luck, for I knew nothing of boxing). He scrambled to his feet and came at me. I poked out with my left and, as luck would have it, caught him strongly enough on the jaw to upset him a second time. He was by no means finished, but got up and tried again. This time, by good luck, or good management, I don't know which, he got his arms around me, caught hold of the bottom of my jacket, which was open, and pulled it up over my head and down over my eyes, so that I couldn't see anything but my feet. I began to be alarmed that he might have *me* down on the floor. I fumbled in my darkness, got my hands on his throat, and forced him to his knees. I let him go. He got up again. I choked him again, and when I asked if he'd had enough, he replied "Yeah, I guess so."

Still heated with battle, I charged into the Principal's office to tell him the story. His first reaction was dismay; then fear – fear that the school might get into trouble. He wanted me to get on the train for Montreal at once, and see the boy's father before the boy did. I was still too angry, however, for counsels of prudence. I said, "I'll do nothing of the kind. To hell with it," and I too, rather like Tom, swaggered noisily out.

The next morning when the school sat down together for breakfast and Tom came in, I was painfully embarrassed. His face was badly swollen, and he had a black eye and a lump on his forehead. He looked as if some great brute had beaten him without mercy. The incident had curious consequences: it gave Tom something of a hero status for standing up to me; it gave me a wholly unexpected reputation as a tough guy, handy with his mitts; and Tom, although he attended class and kept out of trouble, refused to speak to me.

I let this go on for a short time, and then my common sense and a deal of shame took hold of me. I called Tom into my room in the residence and said, "Tom, this is too bad, I have to say that you were badly out of line before our fight began. I can't back away from that. But I'll also say that it was altogether wrong of me to slug you. I'm bigger and older, and stronger. And besides, that's no way to keep order in a school. I'm sorry I hit you. Can we shake hands and be friends?" The good fellow promptly shot out his hand. I was amused and touched when an hour later he returned to ask me if I would play tennis with him; a game, I gather, at which he rather fancied himself. I went over to the courts where I had the satisfaction – and I admit it *was* a satisfaction – of beating him soundly and observing that he took his defeat like a gentleman and a good sport. And that's the end of that story.

The school was not in good shape; certainly the academic department wasn't. Our standards were too low; our record in the provincial matriculation examinations was poor. Discipline was shaky, and the top administration, in which I include myself, was weak. We all lacked a sound sense of direction. But all that was forty-six years ago.

On February 14, 1928, I received a message from the Imperial Order, Daughters of the Empire, New Brunswick Chapter, that I had been awarded an overseas university scholarship. It was a graceful coincidence that I got this delightful message from the women of New Brunswick on St. Valentine's Day. It was so late in the year that I had a difficult time in finding a place at Oxford. But an old Mt. A. friend, Ray Betts, who was on the spot, advised me to send my documents to him, and promised to turn over stones and explore avenues on my behalf. Through his good offices I was admitted to Exeter College, on the Turl, where I showed up in mid-September of the same year.

CHAPTER SIX

Before I left for Oxford I had to settle one very important matter. I had met a girl called Jean Miller at Mt. A. in 1925 and was very much in love with her. I couldn't leave Canada for two years, or perhaps three, without trying to persuade her into a formal engagement. Mr. G.W. Reid, the father of my high-school pal Bruce, was a wholesale jeweller. He told me once, with a knowing smile, that when I had steadied my roving eye sufficiently to justify the purchase of an engagement ring, I was to come to him. I did so. He gave into my care an assortment of half-a-dozen rings, ranging in wholesale price from about eighty-five to a hundred and fifteen dollars. I stuffed them into my pocket and headed for Charlottetown.

I did everything in style. First I whispered my intentions to Jean's mother. Not being rebuffed, I formally asked Mr. Miller – Art – for his daughter's hand. He shook his head, and I began to wonder if I had totally mistaken my standing in the Miller household. But he was not objecting to me or to my proposal; he was questioning the durability of an engagement which was to be followed so abruptly by the young man's departure for foreign shores, with no clearly specified date for his return. He didn't object: he did say, with considerable emphasis, that if Jean put my ring on her finger, she'd damned well better keep it there. I took this firm parental utterance as a strong hint that we'd better not put too much faith in the old adage, "Absence makes the heart grow fonder." I made my proposal to Jean, and being accepted, trotted out my assortment of not very impressive rings. With that unerring taste which, though perhaps not conspicuous in her choice of a fiancé, has always characterized her selection of "objets d'art," she picked out at once the most expensive of the bunch, and undoubtedly the most attractively designed.

Back in Truro, I returned the other rings to G.W. Reid, and found, somehow, the money to pay him. It was a small enough sum, but for a young man starting from scratch, who had to borrow money to get to Oxford, where his first scholarship payment would be made, it was a considerable fraction of his liquid assets. That certainly was the opinion of my father and mother, who showed consternation when they learned what a dashing fellow and heavy spender their younger son had turned out to be. Of course, back then in 1928, money was still valuable.

I have always been conscious of my unpayable debt to Jean: for love returned, for companionship, for understanding me better than I ever understood myself, for unending forgiveness, and for help in a thousand ways as we moved along in a life which has seen its troubles and its modest successes, and which has always been exciting and fulfilling – no doubt more fulfilling for me than for her. To make a wife know that she has an equal share in the "modest successes," as she inescapably has in enduring the "troubles," is something, sadly, that many men are never completely able to do.

In September of 1928 I sailed from Montreal for Southampton. Among the small contingent of young Canadian scholars bound for Oxford and Cambridge on that particular Cunarder, I remember two: Burton Keirstead of UNB and Jack Irving of the University of Toronto. I don't recall much of the voyage except my own valiant attempts to stave off sea-sickness, Burton's abrupt assumption of an English accent, and Jack's confidential information, given to us furtively as he looked about to see that no one else was within hearing, that he had "a scoop in epistemology." At that time I hadn't the slightest idea what epistemology was except that it had some-thing to do with Jack's principal interest philosophy. But I knew what a scoop was, and this combination of journalistic and philoso-phical lingo entertained me hugely and, I suspect, roused my envy. How marvellous to be going to Cambridge with a scoop in episte-mology! God knows I didn't have a scoop in anything. I had only vague notions of what awaited me at Oxford, and a pious determina-tion to do my best at my studies in Eng. Lang. and Lit.; to learn to write decent English prose if I could, and not to let down the women of New Brunswick who had so generously and unexpectedly come up with this wonderful scholarship. Burton was an excellent com-panion. We were close friends all through our Oxford days – he was at my College, Exeter – and long after. Unhappily – and this has occurred several times in my peripatetic life – I lost my friend during his latter years. We drifted apart after he left his post as head of the department of economics at McGill and went to the University of Toronto.

I arrived in Oxford a day or so earlier than I was supposed to, but though my welcome at Exeter was a bit cool because of this circumstance, no one made any trouble for me. Since all the rooms in College had long since been allocated, it was necessary for me to find lodgings, or "digs" at once. The Sub-Rector, Dacre Balsdon, gave me the name of a place in Argyle Street, rather more than a mile out the Iffley Road, where an American Rhodes Scholar had occupied the rooms the previous year. They were now free: the College had just received the dreadful news from Paris that the young man had committed suicide. With another American Rhodes Scholar, Johnnie Ochiltree, I went along to Argyle Street, he to look over the effects of the poor suicide and prepare them for shipment to America; and I to give Johnnie a hand, and to size up the rooms as possible quarters for myself. Word had been received from America that everything, without exception, was to be sent home. Johnnie and I, feeling ourselves to be men of the world, decided not to send back anything which might add to the mother's bewilderment and grief. We found the beginnings of two or three letters which the young man had apparently been writing in some distress, and had been unable to go on with, after a couple of not very coherent opening sentences. Each was directed to the same woman, or girl, in Paris. We destroyed these: on the whole, I think we were right.

This was a sobering introduction to the great University, but I hadn't known the young American, and since the *locus* of the event was Paris and not Oxford, I did not let it upset me or make me uncomfortable about engaging the rooms.

I confess that I responded very quickly to the charm of whatever was ancient by Canadian standards. I suppose it was the ever-present sense that men and women had been here for a long, long time that fascinated me. They had cultivated the soil for centuries, had domesticated almost everything, and placed the stamp of history on so much that one was now going to live with, day by day. Fresh as I was from the newness and the vast distances of Canada, I looked and stared at this old England with feelings of content and of delight – feelings that persist with me today. In fact, I love the country.

It wasn't at all difficult to make the necessary adjustments to the strange environment of Oxford and to certain peculiar customs of the University. I relished my time in Oxford, and look back upon it with gratitude and with awareness that it exercised an enormous and beneficial influence on my life. I was twenty-six when I arrived there, a fact which made me, to the best of my recollection, the old man of the undergraduate population of Exeter.

Admittedly, some things irked me. For one, there was a rule that in the mornings at eight o'clock everyone must attend either chapel or roll-call. Being – as I was astonished to hear myself called – a nonconformist, I elected roll-call. You walked in the door of the room, said "Good morning, Sir," to the Sub-Rector or whichever Don was on duty, gave your name to the scout with the roll in front of him, and walked out another door. Total elapsed time, about eight seconds. For this, I got up early, cycled over a mile to the College, cycled back to Argyle Street for breakfast, and then cycled back again to Exeter. An Indian friend of mine, Hamayun Kabir, who was later to be a minister in Nehru's cabinet, said to me one day, "I say, Trueman, you're quite silly to do this, you know. I went to the Sub-Rector and told him my story, where I lived, and that I'd been through all this as an undergraduate elsewhere, and the man excused me from attending either roll-call or chapel."

I promptly went to see Dacre Balsdon, the Sub-Rector, who was very bored with me, and said in his languid and indifferent way, and in the most extreme Oxford accent I was ever to hear, "Oh, no-er-er-er-Trueman, is it? No exceptions can be made, none whatever. Run along now, do." I couldn't tell him, of course, that he had already made an exception and that I knew about it, lest I put a spoke in Kabir's wheel: he might just possibly have been getting away with something. I swallowed my resentment and kept on attending roll-call, which was merely a device to get undergraduates out of bed betimes in the morning. At the age of twenty-six, after four years of earning my own living, and with a university degree behind me, I felt that I didn't need this childish piece of coercion.

But the little comedy was not yet ended. The next year, when I had rooms in College and had only to cross the Quad to reach roll-call, I got a facetious note from Balsdon, which ran something like this: "Dear Trueman: While looking over some records this morning, I was made aware of your great age. If I were you, I should discontinue the practice of attending roll-call." Damn his eyes!

I can't say that after all these years I harbour resentments against

Balsdon and the College. And yet, and yet – ? It's odd that the most cordial greeting I ever had at Exeter – this was eighteen years after I had gone down – came from the porter. I was attending the Commonwealth University Conference in 1948, a week at Bristol and a second week at Oxford. In Oxford I asked to be put up at my old College. When I first arrived I saw at once that the porter was Jack, whom I well remembered, although he hadn't been my scout. I walked into his cubby-hole, just inside the College doors, and said, "Well, Jack, how are you?" I put out my hand, which he took. His other hand came down over mine as he exclaimed, with apparently genuine pleasure, "Why, it's Mr. Trueman!" Later on during my stay I thought that out of courtesy I should pay my respects to the Rector, E.A. Barbour. I had Jack find out if he was in and would receive my visit. I found his study, knocked at the door, and was told to enter. The Rector was seated at his desk, pen in hand. I told him who I was and what I'd been doing, not neglecting to state that I was *en route*, via Oxford, from the University of Manitoba to the University of New Brunswick, and that I was the new President of the latter and the one-time President of the former. (No doubt it was a little naïve of me to bid for his interest so blatantly.) He said, "Oh yes, I hadn't realized you were here until this morning when I was looking over the list of our conference guests." He didn't rise. He didn't put down his pen. He didn't ask me any questions. He didn't suggest that we might meet later and have a drink and some talk. After a few perfunctory words I got out.

I have never really felt comfortable in Exeter ever since. But I must set the record straight by an admission: on one or two occasions in quite recent years I have received the most cordial hospitality from the Rector, Ken Wheare, now retired. Wheare is a most genial man. The first time I met him, in the 1960's – I forget the exact year – I referred to Diggory Wheare, First Professor of Ancient History in the University of Oxford, and I suggested, half facetiously, that no doubt he was the rector's remote ancestor. He said, "Come along with me," and took me at once to the Chapel where he showed me a stone tablet let into the floor on the north side of the aisle, inscribed to the memory of Digg. Wheare, First Professor, etc. Old Digg was a west-countryman; since Ken Wheare's family came from Devon or Cornwall, there was indeed, I gathered, a distinct possibility that the First Professor of Ancient History in the University of Oxford was a distant progenitor of the man I was talking to.

CHAPTER SEVEN

My tutor at Exeter was Nevill Henry Kendal Aylmer Coghill, who was born in Ireland and brought up in County Cork. His mother's sister was Edith Somerville, joint author of those delightful stories of Irish life, *Experiences of an Irish R.M.* Whatever "appropriate" feelings I have for Exeter College centre about this man. Coghill was young, in his late twenties, when I first knew him. He was scholarly, imaginative, sensitive, sympathetic, witty, and an excellent talker. Easily the best thing that happened to me at Oxford was the regular tutorial session I had with him, once a week for four of the six terms I spent at the University.

It was a great relief to be rid of the burden of lecture attendance. At Mt. Allison, where compulsory attendance was still in force, I went to as many as fifteen lectures a week. But at our first meeting, Coghill advised: "Look over the lecture list for this term and select any that you think may be helpful. But don't go to more than – say – three or four a week. I see Professor so-and-so's name on the list. He's a fine scholar. Try him out. Here's Miss so-and-so, also a good scholar, but you may not wish to take lectures from her. Try her out; if you don't think you're getting anything useful, drop her." This casual, even cavalier treatment of the eminent scholars at Oxford appealed to me no end: during one entire term, finding nothing on the list that I thought deserving of my serious scholarly attention, I attended no lectures at all.

One other welcome difference between Oxford and Mount Allison was that my formal studies at Oxford were confined wholly to English Language and Literature. The young man coming up to Oxford from a public school and electing to read in this or that discipline – say the Honours English School – was not required to "do" an additional course in science, another in political economy, another in a foreign language, and yet another in history. In short, he was not pitched into the kind of miscellaneous program by which, in this country, we produce our B.A.'s. Of course, I *did* study other subjects, notably history and German, and I got on with my music. The program allowed time for these extra-curricular investigations.

The tutorials with Coghill were a pleasure. I always looked forward to them with a strong sense that something interesting, useful, and even exciting was likely to happen during these hours of conversational exchange – which is what they largely were, apart from the fifteen or twenty minutes it took me to read my paper. As I have said, Coghill was an excellent talker. Our conversations, of necessity, covered the particular topics that I had been asked to write on, but they ranged much further afield – to other literatures, to music, to painting and sculpture, to language, to the theatre (he was famous for his production of plays at Oxford: *Hamlet, A Midsummer Night's Dream, Sampson Agonistes, Everyman*, and many others). It strikes me that here, with Coghill in his study, the essential virtue of the system of instruction was realized: this placing of a young student in close, frequent, and sustained relationship with a scholar of wide interests, a good conversationalist with a sense of humour, sympathetic with youth, who obviously didn't regard his tutorial duties as an unavoidable and disagreeable condition of his employment, to be met and discharged as quickly and perfunctorily as circumstances would allow, but as a pleasure and an opportunity.

In 1966, Faber and Faber published *To Nevill Coghill from Friends*. The occasion was Nevill's retirement as Merton Professor of English Literature. He had moved from Exeter to Merton College many years after I went down. The book, as the blurb explains, is "not in any sense an academic *Festschrift*." It contains personal tributes and some scholarly pieces by friends and former pupils, among them Glynne Wickham, Cleanth Brooks (who was "up" with me at Exeter) and W.H. Auden, who though at Christ Church, came to Coghill for his Eng. Lit. tutorials. I have the book beside me; here is one of Auden's stanzas, which says so much better than I can what Nevill meant to his pupils:

> endowed with the charm
> of your Irish provenance
> but no proper-false,
> you countenanced all species,

the alphas, the bone-
idle, the obstreperous
and the really rum,
never looked cross or sleepy
when our essays were
more about ourselves than Chaucer,
and no unfinished
shy production felt afraid
to knock on your door.

(From *To Professor Nevill Coghill
upon his retirement, in A.D. 1966*)

Nevill Coghill sent me a little book in July, 1950. I had sent him the printed copy of an address on Language I had given to a meeting of lawyers in Saint John, N.B.. He was good enough to write me about it and to make use of these words: "I do not think I have ever published anything that I re-wrote less than four times....It is a sweat and a joy – but when it is at last in print it has the simplicity I would like. In fact I am best pleased when anything I have written seems as easy and simple as casual talk. Your speech had this quality in every line and was a pleasure to read apart from the value of the philosophy in it, if such a distinction can be made."

The book he sent me was *The Masque of Hope*, written by him to celebrate the visit of HRH Princess Elizabeth to University College, 25 May, 1948. It was performed by the Oxford University Dramatic Society. On the flyleaf Nevill wrote "A.W. Trueman, with proud and happy memories of our work together at Oxford." Not, you will notice, "the work he did for me," but "our work together." This says a good deal about what kind of tutor he was.

For part of my first Christmas holidays I "Ryderized." Lady Frances Ryder, helped by the kind offices of her many friends, had long made it a practice to provide vacation hospitality to overseas students. I remember going to a huge tea party, in Oxford, and being asked by Lady Frances if I should like to visit an English house for a week or more, and if so, where in England I should like to go. I answered "Yes, thank you, very much," to her first question, and "Devon, if possible," to her second. The upshot of this was that a month or so later I found myself getting off the train at Exeter, and being met by a uniformed chauffeur, who drove me, in a magnificent car, to St. Mary Church, just outside the city, and to the home of Mrs. Armitage-Rhodes. Mrs. Armitage-Rhodes, a Canadian by birth, had lived in England much of her life. She was a widow, with a beautiful house, and two agreeable and friendly daughters who did everything in their power to make my stay pleasant.

After being welcomed cordially by my hostess I asked her – this was very late in the afternoon – if I should dress for dinner. She told me that ordinarily the family didn't dress, but this evening she was giving a small dinner party – more or less in my honour, I supposed – for a few young people of the neighbourhood, and that black tie would be in order. Relieved to know the drill, I went to my room. Someone had opened up my luggage and distributed my modest belongings in various appropriate places. (Home, I thought, was never like this.) But as I was dressing, I was mortified to discover that I'd left my black tie and cuff links and shirt studs behind. What to do? I called a maid and explained my difficulty, and a minute or two later, I heard the clickety-click of high heels coming along the hall. My hostess appeared in the doorway, looking very mirthful indeed, and dangling between thumb and fore-finger a tiny piece of black ribbon about eight or nine inches long and half-an-inch wide – the only article in the entire household, she gave me to understand, that even remotely resembled a gentleman's black tie.

I took the damned thing back into my room, faced the mirror, and went to work. It was far too short to go round my neck. I buttoned my dress shirt at the top, pushed one end of the ribbon down over the top button, between it and my neck, then underneath it, and back through to the front. I thus got the two ends of the thing in my hands. I could now make a bow-knot, which I did, a wee thing less than two inches long. But the position of this pathetic piece of millinery was exactly vertical. By dint of squeezing and pulling and torturing the bow I finally got it to sit at an angle of forty-five degrees. For cuff links and shirt studs I used brass collar-buttons which, thank God, I found in my kit. And that's the way I appeared at my first formal dinner party in an English home, with my tiny tie pointing northeast-southwest, and my bosom dotted with brass. But halfway through dinner there arrived another "Ryderizer," correctly clad; a chap from Australia, who had landed at Southampton early that afternoon. As we left the table, I clutched his arm and said, "For God's sake, have you got another black tie?" Luck was with me: he'd just bought a new one, which he was wearing, and the old one was in his room, and at my disposal.

Before the Easter recess of 1929 I got in touch with a student agency in London to inquire if I could arrange to visit a German family for a few weeks. I wanted to see something of life in a German city, to expand my knowledge and improve my use of the language. The agency put me in touch with the Sigmund Feuchtwangers, in Munich, on Grillpartzer Strasse. They agreed to take me in, and were so kind as to let me know that my arrival in Munich would coincide with the opening of the Wagner-Mozart Opera Festival. They would get tickets for me if I was interested, but I would have to send money in advance because they themselves had very little to spare. I sent off some pounds at once.

The Feuchtwangers proved to be delightful people, a Jewish couple with a charming little boy, Hans. They lived in a comfortable apartment filled with books and pictures. Herr Feuchtwanger, I learned, was first cousin to Leon Feuchtwanger, the author of *Jew-Süss*. I remember that my host told me, after we had become acquainted and were on easy terms, that he was desperately afraid of the quickly developing anti-Semitism in Munich. This was early in 1929, ten years before the Second World War broke out. I was made welcome and comfortable. I made some progress with my German, not unmarked by comical blunders which amused my host and hostess, although their kindly laughter never embarrassed me.

My first ticket was for a performance of Wagner's *Parsifal* in the Opera House just across the Square. Apart from Gilbert and Sullivan's *Trial by Jury*, which I had seen (heard?) in Montreal the night before I sailed for England, this was my very first opera – if it's permissible even to name *Trial by Jury* in this connection. My friends, at least those who know something about opera, are always amused when they learn that *Parsifal* was my introduction to this great art form. The performance lasted for about six hours, with intervals for the ingestion of beer and wurst, and other relief. I didn't understand much of it, although I had provided myself with an outline of the plot. But the singing was magnificent, and the sets, and the theatre itself, splendid, and I had an unforgettable evening.

To descend from the sublime to the nearly ridiculous, I relate another incident which struck me most forcibly after my return to

Exeter. A young English friend, one day having reasons of his own – unknown to his friends – for celebration, began to drink beer before noon and continued throughout lunch, with the unfortunate consequence that by two o'clock he was pleasantly drunk. He made the mistake which one should carefully avoid in Oxford – the mistake of drawing attention to oneself. He wandered unsteadily about the Quad, singing little songs; he ventured out on the grass-plot, which was forbidden country. He was reported to the Sub-Rector, Balsdon, who, I admit, handled this little disciplinary problem superbly. After rebuking Blaggers, he fined him a guinea, the going price of minor sin at that time. As Blaggers turned to leave, the Sub-Rector spoke again, saying, as Blaggers reported it: "I want you to understand very clearly why I am fining you a guinea. I'm not fining you a guinea for being drunk; I'm fining you a guinea for being drunk *in the afternoon.*"

I was tremendously impressed by this subtle distinction, which conveyed to my astonished Mount Allison mind the idea that the College was quite prepared, without in any way condoning drunkeness, to be tolerant of youthful exuberance in the evening, after the day's work had presumably been looked to; but that being drunk in the afternoon, when one should either be studying or engaged in healthful games, was irresponsible and degenerate behaviour, something that no gentleman should be guilty of, and that the College would not tolerate. I see very little reason to quarrel with this principle, or with the Sub-Rector's action in this particular case.

CHAPTER EIGHT

At the end of my second year at Oxford I received an offer from Mount Allison of an assistant professorship in the Department of English. Uncle George, who wrote the letter, insisted that he had refused to take part in the discussion which preceded the offer. Professor Tweedie had made the proposal to the Board of Governors and had carried it through. The salary was to be $1,900. Shortly after I had gratefully accepted the offer, another arrived, from United College in Winnipeg, at a salary of $2,100. I informed Uncle George of this, with no suggestion that I intended to back off from Mount A. The good man promptly wrote me again, raising the salary to $2,100: he did not think, he said, that I should be penalized for my loyalty.

I began my duties in September of 1930. Professor Tweedie gave me a warm welcome and a chair opposite his at the only desk in the little office. It was an exciting experience to stand and deliver to my first university class, Freshman English. This was a course I had not taken as an undergraduate, since I entered Mt. A. in 1924 as a Freshie-Soph, i.e., as a second-year student with credits from Nova Scotia for all my first-year subjects. Before I could safely be let loose on the Freshmen it was necessary for Professor Tweedie to give me a detailed summary of his strategy and tactics, not only because I was unfamiliar with the content of the course, but because I was not to teach it independently: I was to take over one of the two sections into which, only a year or two earlier, it had at last been divided. This division of duties put me in direct competition, as it were, with my senior. His advantage in superior knowledge, experience, and skill was somewhat offset by my advantage in youth, freshness (if that's not an ambiguous word), and my recent arrival from Oxford. To my embarrassment, some students tried openly to get into my section at registration time, or to be transferred to it later on. But my old Professor handled this nonsense with good nature, and, I suspect, amusement. I couldn't have been introduced to my new work under more genial and more encouraging auspices.

In those remote days, we gave much attention to grammar, logic (not of course in the formal sense) and rhetoric; the mediaeval trivium, in fact. We taught our students sentence and paragraph construction, since they hadn't been well coached in these matters before. We insisted that they know something of metrics and figures of speech. We had them read a selection of essays, short stories, poems, and plays. We required them to write a short essay – say, three or four hundred words – every week, and we carefully read and criticized them all. I soon learned many things that Professor Tweedie had discovered over long years. For instance, I found out that a large proportion of the Freshmen couldn't write a page of prose that was readable and avoided the commission of gross violence on the English language. Even then, over forty-five years ago, teachers were beginning to appear who were convinced that the walls could be erected and the roof put on the house without first laying the foundations. In my opinion, the consequences of this type of pedagogy have grown steadily worse.

I wrestled with these teaching problems at Mt. A., sometimes very impatiently, I'm afraid, from 1930 to 1942. Professor Tweedie continued as the head of our little department for seven years after my return from Oxford. He retired after an even half-century of service to his Alma Mater. Before he left he had taught the sons and daughters of his former students and possibly even their grandchildren. That service was of incalculable value to Mount Allison. He was an excellent scholar though not a researcher and writer; his lectures were always lucid and his manner dignified – in the best sense of that word. He had what I have called a dry mind; he was logical and rather unemotional in his presentation of literature, and he laid great stress on "knowing what the man said." In our study of Shakespeare, for example, he insisted that we acquire a good working knowledge of Shakespearean English, that we look up the difficult words and struggle with passages that weren't immediately clear to us.

Professor Tweedie stood for scholarship, for integrity, for dignity, and for the rational disciplined life. I recall with pleasure that he gave me one of the first drinks, if not the very first, that I ever had at Mount Allison. (It was a very small drink.) My wife and I were making a social call at the cottage where he lived with his sister, Leora. "P.T." (one of his nicknames) retired to the kitchen and shortly returned bearing a tray on which rested four very small glasses. The drink was porter, which, we were given to understand, was to be sipped as if it were a liqueur. But what I remember most vividly about this little episode is the twinkle in his eye when he appeared with his treat, and the subtly conveyed sense of mischief and daring with which he contrived to invest this departure from the official conventions of Mount Allison's social behaviour.

"P.T." retired in 1937. The University was always hard up for money. Salaries were shockingly low. The library grants for departmental use were pitiful. Support for research was at a minimum. It was under these circumstances that I was made head of the department – Uncle George, the President, again refusing to take part in the preliminary discussions. A few months before, I had a "feeler" from Queen's University, and I went to Kingston to have a talk with Principal Wallace and a few others. Queen's wanted someone to administer and give life to their program of adult education, much of which was conducted by correspondence. To tell the truth I wasn't at all interested in the post, after I found out what it was. Furthermore, the Vice-Principal – MacNeil, I think was his name – advised me in a private conversation to leave it alone. "It's not for you," he said. Very soon, I indicated that there was no point in going on with the discussion, and the matter was dropped. It wasn't until after Professor Tweedie's death a few years later that the President, Uncle George, felt free to tell me of "P.T.'s" concern about my dallying with Queen's. "P.T." was due to retire about this time on a pension, after half a century of service, of fifteen hundred dollars a year. He went to Uncle George and said that it would be a great mistake to let Albert go, and offered to contribute five hundred dollars a year, a third of his pension, if a salary increase of that amount would make the difference between keeping me at Mt. A. and losing me. I'm happy to say that his offer was not accepted. It is no wonder that I recall him with respect and gratitude and affection: admired teacher, beloved colleague, generous and faithful friend. When he died, a note attached to his will indicated that he wished me to be given the desk-table in his study at the cottage, the large rug on the sitting-room floor, the Century Dictionary (10 vols.), Chambers English Literature (3 vols.), and a group of "poets" on a designated shelf in his library. I now have the books on *my* shelves where from time to time I come across his copy of Milton, or Tennyson, or Browning, containing little interleaved scraps of paper on which his handwriting appears.

During my twelve years in the department I spent far too much time in Gilbert and Sullivan opera. Harold Hamer, the head of the Conservatory of Music, was extremely skilful in the production of G. and S. and I found it impossible to stand out against the pressure to take part, from Hamer and many others. Since there weren't many baritones about the place, to refuse a role was generally looked upon as selfish, unaccommodating, and not in accord with what we fondly conceived to be our special Mt. A. spirit. Consequently I sang and clowned my way through *H.M.S. Pinafore* (twice), *The Mikado* (twice), *Iolanthe*, *The Gondoliers*, *The Pirates of Penzance*, and *Patience*. When I think of the antics I performed on the stage of Fawcett Hall and the time I spent in preparing for them, I feel slightly ashamed. Of course, except for the drag of rehearsal after rehearsal, I enjoyed myself hugely, being something of an egotist and something of a ham actor. One thing the operas did for me was to keep me singing. The vocalism needed was not as rigorous as that required by German Lieder and Handelian oratorio, but still they kept me in shape, and from that fact there emerged one of the most exciting weeks of my life.

A very interesting German baritone, Ernst Wolff, came to the campus for a concert and helpful sessions with senior vocal students. He was a fine musician and a friendly man. My coach, Cecil Blanchard Selfridge – to whom I owe a great deal – had me sing for Wolff, who was sufficiently impressed to urge me to go to New York, where, he said, I should arrange for lessons with the best Lieder coach in North America, Conrad Bos.

The next summer I registered for certain English courses at Columbia and, the way having been prepared for me by a letter from Wolff, went to see Conrad Bos. He received me with a Dutch compatriot, Wilhelm Van Giesen, who did voice coaching, I believe, at the Juillard School of Music. They listened to me sing and then talked to me for half an hour. Their verdict was that I had an excellent voice, that I was very musical, that my education, greatly superior to that of most singers, was a distinct advantage, and that undoubtedly I could become a professional singer. But they said that in New York there were a great many talented young singers who couldn't get enough engagements to make a living. Their advice was that I work with them for the six or seven weeks I had free, go back

57

to my job as head of the Mt. A. Department of English, and use my singing as an avocation rather than as a profession. I thought this was very sensible, as well as gratifying.

After a few lessons in repertoire with Bos, he said: "Mr. Trueman, I could certainly be of help to you for the next few weeks in your study of German Lieder, but you are musical and approach a song with musical intelligence and insight. It would be a far better investment of your money and limited time to work solely with Van Giesen on voice production." So off I went to Van Giesen six days a week. He worked me hard and I made quick improvement. About the beginning of the fifth week, he said, "You remember the talk you had with Mr. Bos and me, and the advice we gave you?" Indeed I did, I said, and added that I thought their judgment was sound. He then electrified me by saying, "But I have changed my mind! I think you can become a very, very successful professional singer. If you could come to New York for a year and study with us we could then arrange a European tour, and on your return, Mr. Bos, with his connections, could easily get you an audition at the 'Met.'"

I was bowled over. For a week I walked the sidewalks of New York in something of a daze. But common sense prevailed: for one thing I had no money; for another I had a family to support; and for a third, I was over thirty years old, and that's pretty late to gamble on a new and chancey career. So I put it all behind me.

The final episode in this little adventure was comical. Back at Mt. A., I told Uncle George all about my adventure. He nodded gravely and in satisfaction, and said, "I'm very glad you made that decision. After all" – and here he spoke with fine Victorian distaste – "it would have been almost like going on the stage." One isn't raised a Methodist for nothing!

Among the various duties that I assumed during those twelve years at Mt. A. was the "Deanship" of the men's residence. After Dr. Bigelow came to the conclusion that he'd had enough of it – and how he stood it for ten years or more I can't imagine – the University asked me to take over. This meant that Jean and I – we had been married on June 8, 1931 – moved into the Dean's apartment on the second floor at one end of the long building, and took our meals in the huge dining-room in the basement. This was as ugly a room as could have been conceived by anyone determined to debase the art of dining, and encourage the utmost rapidity of entrance, food consumption, and exit. It was plain and bare, with a low ceiling which supported a tangle of water pipes, steam pipes, and Heaven knows what else. The furniture was of the kitchen variety. The waiters, students working their way through college, served the food as swiftly as possible to the undergrads, often speeding up the process by throwing – I mean, literally, throwing – bread and other throwable items of food from the serving end of the table to the other. It was, of course, to their advantage to get the job done as quickly as possible in order to clear the way for their morning and afternoon labs and lectures. Good table manners were generally scorned. There seemed to be nothing that one could do about these deplorable customs. I had myself gone through this as an undergraduate, with resignation but without any unconquerable sense of dismay. But as the Dean of the place, I often thought of my Oxford days when meals were served by the College servants in Exeter's beautiful hall, with its high, beamed ceilings, its portraits of ancient worthies, and its fine oak screen; with the dons at high table, on a dais two or three feet above the Hall's floor level, serving as a check on any undergraduate exuberance that tended to express itself *too* coarsely.

The residence was run under a system of student government, for the initiation of which Bigelow was largely responsible. On the whole, it worked very well. Once a week I met with the Council, and with them discussed and ruled on any disciplinary problems which had arisen, dealt with the monotonously recurring complaints about the food, and tried to ward off what I thought were unwise and dangerous attempts to increase the laxity of residence *mores* – and God knows, they were already lax enough. I tried to be understanding and tolerant, and by my understanding and tolerance I got myself into minor trouble.

It was the Mt. A. rule that liquor must not be owned or consumed on the campus; not that the rule prevented its possession and use by either faculty or students. In the residence the boys sometimes became a little too careless. One Spring, as convocation week approached, I met with the "inmates" in Eurhetorian Hall for a general talk. Among the inspired things that I said – to great applause – was something like this: "Now, Convocation Week is upon us. Visitors in scores, your fathers and mothers in fact, will be roaming about the campus and prowling about in the buildings, this one included. As you well know, you are not supposed to drink in the residence or elsewhere, and I strongly urge you not to do so. But if you insist on breaking the regulations, will you please be considerate enough not to bowl your empty beer bottles down the second floor corridor and pile them up in a smashed, conspicuous heap against the door of the Dean's apartment!" (Roars of laughter.) This seemed to me a reasonable plea – "with it" if you like. But of course the report of the Dean's remarks was soon tossed about the campus, and came to the eager ears of "Clem" Avard, member of the Board of Regents, and publisher of the Sackville *Tribune*, and shortly I had to defend myself against the allegation that I was taking a very lax view of the University's temperance laws, and by my good humour and easy discipline was in fact encouraging the students to drink. No doubt I had been naïve.

After a comparatively short tour of duty as Dean of the men's residence – I forget the exact number of years – Jean and I moved out to a pleasant cottage known as the Campbell House. We spent several years there.

The most important events of my twelve years in Sackville were my marriage with Jean, and the arrivals, suitably spaced, of our two children, William Peter Main and Sara (Sally) Keillor. Jean faced her confinement apparently quite unperturbed: I can make no such claim for myself. On Christmas Day, 1934, we had planned a breakfast party for a few University friends. About seven o'clock that morning Jean decided it would be wise of her to make tracks at once for Mrs. Bern Bowser's nursing home, where we had prudently reserved a room. Off she went in a taxi – she wouldn't let me go with her – and I set about preparing the breakfast.

Later in the morning, after ten, our friends began to drift in. Over and over again I explained the absence of the hostess; again and again I telephoned the nursing home, until I provoked Mrs. Bowser into replying, with a touch of exasperation, "Don't call us. We'll call you." There was nothing for me to do but busy myself with "the eggs and the ham and the strawberry jam," and attempt to entertain our guests.

We breakfasted in leisurely fashion, everyone but the prospective father ostensibly at ease and self-consciously festive. Later – it seemed *much* later to me – while I was still renewing supplies of toast and coffee, tossing eggs into the skillet, and trying to make lucid conversation, the telephone rang between twelve and twelve-thirty. Peter had arrived in the exact middle of things, where, for Jean and me, he has pretty constantly remained. As I look back, it seems to have been no time before we'd started him off to school, and he was playing the usual games that little boys play, getting into the usual troubles, and rejoicing his parents in the usual unusual ways.

Sally came along on November 19, 1938, arriving at the inconvenient hour of four in the morning – no breakfast-interrupter or scene-stealer. We nearly lost Sally when she was still a baby. One afternoon she suddenly began to choke; her breathing became a struggle and her face grew purple. I tried everything I could think of – putting an exploratory finger down her throat; even holding her up by the heels and spanking her back and little bottom. It was no use. The only doctor available, Ed Barnhill, was out on rounds, but his nurse, at our call, telephoned here and there until she reached him. He came on the run, quickly found the trouble, and with clever hands swabbed the mucus from her throat, undoubtedly saving her life, and restoring to reasonable calm her terrified parents. Without any more narrow escapes from infant disasters, she quickly grew into beautiful childhood, the enchantress of the early years of our married life.

Our children have been a blessing to us. Neither has ever moved far enough away to be out of touch, or to threaten the unity of the family. They have given us six grand-children, all well and strong and in our opinion, intelligent and good-looking and, to our comfort and delight, generous and loving.

In 1938 we made a great decision: to build a house. I had no money, even for a modest down-payment. My salary was then three thousand dollars a year. How we thought we could manage this major financial operation I don't know. But it all worked out. We found an excellent lot, for which we paid nine hundred dollars. Bern Bowser was the contractor. My guess is that Bern built two or three houses every year, not on any speculative basis or with the hope of making even a reasonable profit, but merely to keep busy and provide himself with good wages. It's only by some such supposition that I can account for the low price he gave us. The whole thing – lot, house, and modest landscaping – came to a little less than seven thousand dollars. For that we got, downstairs, a large living-room with fireplace; a pine-panelled study for me, with fireplace, a good dining-room, kitchen, an extra maid's bedroom tacked on to the kitchen, and a small lavatory; upstairs we got a master-bedroom with a huge walk-in closet, three other bedrooms, a beautiful bathroom, a linen closet, and a kind of all-purpose repository over the kitchen and its attached bedroom. Outside we got a one-car garage. The house was solidly built, and the exterior clad in large Douglas fir shingles. I borrowed most of the money from my former landlord, who owned the Campbell House. The Royal Bank helped a little. We moved in just before the War, in 1939.

CHAPTER NINE

In 1942 I had a "feeler," from Saint John, N.B.. The city needed a new Superintendent for the School System. I went down to Saint John to have a look. After an amicable discussion during the course of which I held out for a salary of $4,500, 25 per cent higher than their first offer, I returned to Sackville, pretty certain that the matter would be dropped. To my surprise I received, in a few days, a telephoned offer of the position, and on my terms. I accepted, not without hearing some disapproving words from Uncle George, who said that he didn't want to lose me, and that in going to Saint John I was burying myself in a position which he felt would be extremely difficult and would lead nowhere. We sold the house, at too low a price, and prepared to end my association of more than fifteen years with Mt. Allison.

I moved into my new position as Superintendent of the Saint John City School System on July 1, 1942. The headquarters building was old, rather shabby, and not adequate for the purposes it had to serve. But the building was the least of my immediate worries. Our roster of teachers was about twenty short, and the opening of the next school term was only a few weeks off. To fill these vacancies and fill them fast, I interviewed over seventy applicants, day after day. I had no special training for this job, no degree from Teachers' College, Columbia University, then the mecca for specialists in education. My interviews were conducted solely by the light of nature; using whatever common sense I had. I made full notes: where these young teachers came from, how old they were, what schooling and professional training they had, where and how long they had taught, the quality of their recommendations, their widely differing looks and personalities. After nearly three weeks of assessment of the applicants, I put a list together and took it to a meeting of the Board of School Trustees.

The meeting started smoothly enough, and my first three or four recommendations were accepted without question or comment. But then the Chairman interrupted me:

"I don't recognize that name! Where does she come from?" I consulted my notes, and reported that she came – let's say – from Moncton, had gone through the Normal School at Fredericton, and had taught for three years in Sussex.

"That will never do! The people of Saint John won't stand for it!"

The cat was out of the bag! I was given to understand that the Board hired teachers only if they had been born in Saint John, or had lived there for many years, and had attended the city schools. I was asked if I had any other "foreigners" on my list. I couldn't give a firm answer because, not having known the policy, I hadn't paid much attention to birth-places. The Board decided that the new Superintendent would reconsider his list, and bring it back to a later meeting.

Next day, the *Telegraph Journal* gave most of its back page to the story: "Superintendent's recommendations turned down by School Trustees." Uncle George, very angry, telephoned from Mount Allison. "What are they trying to do to you down there?" Finding some amusement in this reversal of our former roles, I advised *him* to be patient, for all would yet be well. After I had time to think about the Board meeting, I was convinced that the Trustees had put themselves on the spot, not me. Now that the Chairman had brought the hiring practice out into the open where, I gathered, it had never been before, the Trustees, I thought, would surely see that such a ridiculous policy could not stand the light of day. So it proved. When I brought back my list, which I had altered scarcely at all, I refrained from rubbing in the obvious: the pure selfishness of the policy, and the dangers of sustained inbreeding. Instead, I proposed for the Trustees' consideration that the Superintendent could not be expected to recommend inferior teachers simply because they came from Saint John. I further proposed that it was highly unlikely that on a list of – say – seventy teachers, from all over the Province, the Saint John applicants would invariably be superior. I proposed, therefore, a policy I could live with: when in my consideration of two teachers, one from Saint John, and one not, I found the Saint John teacher at least equal to the other in qualifications, or superior, I would recommend her or him; when I did not, I would not. This proposal was accepted, as, when you think about it, it had to be. I carried on for the next three years without ever again being challenged on this issue, and without, I confess, paying much heed to the policy I had secured.

I liked Saint John, and I liked my job. The teachers received me cordially, and refrained from pushing difficulties at me until I had settled in. One of the first things I did was to take a good look at the salary scale. Why on earth would the seventy teachers I had just interviewed want to work in Saint John? The scale was past belief, or would have been if it hadn't lain there on my desk, staring me in the face. It was too late to do anything about the 1942-43 salaries. I haven't got the figures for the scale of that year in my possession, but I'm sure that the salary for a beginning teacher in the elementary schools, Grades one to eight, was in the vicinity of $500. Every beginning teacher had to serve a three-year probationary period before becoming eligible for an increase of $50. Furthermore, if a teacher came into the Saint John system from outside, credit was given for only half the number of years he or she had taught. For example, if a young woman had taught for four years in Moncton, and then was hired in Saint John, she was credited with two years of experience, leaving a third year of her probationary period to be served. I went to the Chairman of the Board of Trustees, Dr. Curran, a jolly, friendly man, and asked him on what grounds the Board justified this iniquitous probation system. His response was ready and unabashed: "We do it to save money." It was so difficult to pry funds out of the city fathers that the Board adopted whatever expedients it could to make ends meet. The teachers were bound to be the principal sufferers. I went to work on the salary scale at once.

According to documents which Dr. B.L. McCarthy, the present Superintendent, has kindly sent me, I was proposing in December 1943 a schedule which would give beginning teachers $700., with an increase of $50. in each of their second and third years, and provide them in their fourth year with a dizzy leap from $800. to $1,150. Apparently this was adopted, since in September of 1944 I had a schedule passed which provided a beginning salary of $800. followed by $50. increases in the second and third years, and a leap to $1,250. in the fourth. On this magnificent salary scale, a male teacher would earn $1,900. after fifteen years of service, and a female teacher $1,600. For the High School the salaries were a bit larger, but not much: in August, we started teachers (female) at $1,000. for those with the lowest class of licence, and at $1,050. and $1,100. for those with higher licences. The men started at the same rates. But *after twenty-six years of service*, the salaries for the women were $1,800., $1,850. and $1,900. and for the men $2,400., $2,450., and $2,500. The incredible fact is that, according to this schedule, after twenty-six years, a woman would be earning only $800. a year more than when she started, and the man only $1,400. more; that is to say, the women would be given an average annual increase of $30.80, and the men, of $53.85.

Shame apparently overtook us, or what is more likely, we received a protest from the teachers, for three months later, in November, Dr. Lunney moved, and the Board agreed, that the differential between the men's and the women's salaries in this schedule be reduced from $600. to $400. Big deal! Even after making allowance for the greater value of money over three decades ago, these salaries certainly were not fair to the teachers. But I succeeded in alleviating some of the evils of the situation, and in letting the teachers know they had a friend at court, and might hope for improvements in other ways.

One of my most interesting responsibilities was inspecting the schools. The Board had never dreamed of supplying the Superintendent with a car, and I didn't have one of my own. A few of the schools were within walking distance of my office, but to reach many of them I had to use the street cars – a slow and tedious business. In the schools I did my best to shed any official manner I might have acquired, and make my visits easy, cheerful, and unportentous. The children were even more interesting than the teachers. In the higher grades, six up to twelve, the pupils had learned their little lessons about authority and the wielders thereof – teachers, principals, and, of course, the Superintendent. They met me with nervous phenomena ranging from giggles and downcast eyes to dismay. But in the lower grades all was different. I recall "inspecting" a Grade three class. As I walked down the aisle, a little girl lifted her face to me when I came near her desk. There was no fear, embarrassment, or nervousness in her frank gaze – only acceptance. At once I had the conviction that nothing, absolutely nothing, stood between her spirit and mine. I stopped at her desk and said, "What are you doing this afternoon?" "I'm drawing a house. See?" And she showed me her drawing with the utmost simplicity, with unclouded welcome and, I felt, with complete assurance that I genuinely wanted to see it. The incident stayed with me all day, diverting my attention from school supplies, janitor service, and critical observation of pedagogical methods – not that I knew much about the latter.

A great many years later I found George Johnston's poem, *No Way Out*, the third stanza of which catches my mood and the meaning of that encounter with great simplicity and purity:

I have not
   Seen Paradise, nor its trees
But what
   I glimpse of unspoiled brings me to my knees.

As the Superintendent of the School System, I didn't often have dealings with the pupils. On one occasion, however, I was directly approached by a High School student who was in very serious trouble. He had been convicted of stealing a typewriter. He had spent a few days in jail: on his release, the Principal had refused permission for him to rejoin his class. The boy came to me in despair, pleading for my intervention. If I would get him back into school, he wouldn't let me down – over and over he assured me. His earnestness and his sincere wish to continue his schooling determined me to help him. I wanted, too, to say something that would give him courage and, if possible, a point of view that would sustain him in what was bound to be an extremely difficult situation. I said, "You say that you won't let me down. Letting *me* down is not really very important. But there *is* someone whom it is very important that you don't let down. Do you know who that is?" He made no answer. "The one you mustn't let down is the next chap who gets into trouble and needs a second chance. As you know only too well, the Principal and the teachers don't want to admit you. If I put you back in your class, and you get into trouble again, and don't study, and fail your year, they are all going to say, 'We told you so.' But if you behave yourself properly and study hard, it will mean that the next fellow who needs a helping hand will probably get it. The teachers will say, 'Remember Joe? He did all right. Let's give Bill another chance.'" Whether or not I was in any degree responsible for Joe's successful year I can't say, but I like to remember that I was able to help him when he so sorely needed it.

My Peter and Sally found it a little awkward to be identified as the children of the Superintendent. I had to be careful, when I inspected their classes, not to betray by word, look or gesture this unfortunate relationship. Sally, at five or six, was too young to be greatly bothered by her father's occasional appearance on the scene, or to suspect that other children might be watching closely for signs of favoured treatment. But Peter, at nine or ten years, had already suffered his little disillusionments about the even charity of his classmates. To my delight, however, he early demonstrated that he had a protective sense of humour and the capacity to make his point of view quite clear, now and then, by a surprisingly mature use of language.

One Saturday noon, after a rather unhappy morning, the family was having lunch. I made a well-intentioned effort to soften the general ill-temper: "Well, Peter, what are your plans for the rest of the day?" "I'm going over to Warwick Gilbert's, and his father's going to take us for a drive up the river." Then in the horrible, condescending and sarcastic manner which parents should never use, I said, "Well! That will eliminate *one* troublesome factor from the development of our afternoon." Peter looked coldly at his father, mother, and sister, and replied, "It'll 'liminate *three* of 'em for me." Peace was restored, and I reflected that the boy had brains, a tongue, and a sense of dry humour that could only be of great advantage to him in his adult years.

A Saint John phenomenon that gave me great pleasure was my morning route to the office, which took me along King Street East. Several side streets open off King and lead down to the Bay of Fundy. On many days, when the old fog-maker was busy, the on-shore breeze pushed the heavy mist up from the harbour and into King Street, across my path. It came out ahead of me, from the side streets, at short intervals, as if from some gigantic pipe-smoker way off to my left. As I walked through these little clouds, the look of them, the smell of them, and the cool, damp feel of them established for me, again and again, the sea personality of the old city. This little experience, I felt, stood for something at the heart of Saint John: it was local, highly individual, *sui generis*. Saint John is perhaps not thought to be a conventionally beautiful city. In fact it has been sneered at, in my time, by writers from "Upper Canada" and the West, writers who should have known better, writers who convicted themselves, not only of discourtesy, but of insensitivity.

The city is filled with interest and excitement, and with its own special beauty for the artist, as Miller Brittain and my old friend Jack Humphrey well knew, and indeed for anyone who lives there for a while and takes the pains to look about him and lay himself open to the appeal of its personality: the two harbours, the steep streets, the unexpected vistas of the Harbour and the Bay, the Market Slip (now, alas, done away with), the old covered market, the houses built right against the sidewalks, on solid rock, the Loyalist reminders, like the old cemetery; the great river, the fog and the resonant, echoing fog-horn; the varying effects of light over the city and the water; the people. You don't find all this in a hasty stop-over between trains, but it's there for those who are capable of feeling it, and are willing to make a modest investment of time, and have an inclination to receive.

I recall other incidents during my visits to the schools. One day as I listened at the back of a room, a little boy was at the blackboard doing a simple problem in arithmetic. I was startled to hear the teacher say, "That's fine, Jimmy. You kin take yer seat now. You done real good!" The lady was deeply embedded in the system after years and years of service. It proved quite useless to protest to the Trustees that this sample of speech was harmfully below the standard we had a right to expect.

Two other incidents that took place in Saint John had nothing to do with my work as the Superintendent. I have never been much of a writer of letters to newspapers, but during the War, and while I was still at Mt. A., I sent a few to the Saint John *Telegraph Journal*, and I sent off one or two after I took up my post in the city. It was this fact, no doubt, that encouraged the editor of the *Telegraph Journal* to ask me to contribute an editorial now and then, which I did.

The principal owner of the paper was Howard Robinson, a rich and influential man in New Brunswick; a charmer, but with lots of steel in his backbone. He asked me to come down to the T.J. building one day, for a purpose which he didn't disclose until I met with him and the General Manager, Tom Drummie. Robinson took the floor. The incumbent editor, he informed me, was about to retire. The paper was going to need a new man. He suggested that I resign as soon as I conveniently could from the Superintendency of the School System, and come to the paper for an indoctrination and training period that could last as long as I saw fit. The paper would send me here and there, with a journalist's credentials, so that I could get my finger on the pulse of things in the newspaper world. I could go to Ottawa, if I wished, sit in the Press Gallery and become acquainted at first hand with what was going on at the national level. When I felt that I was ready to assume the role of editor, I would be properly set up in office, and paid much more than the City paid me for looking after the schools.

Of course I was flattered, but I knew from the start that I didn't want to edit the *Telegraph Journal*, particularly under my friend Tom Drummie, a tough, exacting man, who would expect the new editor to do and write pretty much as he was told; furthermore I was sure I detected some unease on Tom's part, and I suspected that Howard Robinson had "jumped the gun" without waiting to persuade his General Manager of the wisdom of this move; and I knew, too, that I wasn't cut out for an editorial job. I asked for time to think about the offer.

I went home and talked the matter over with Jean. She thought exactly as I did. The only little problem I had was to draft a letter of refusal that would be courteous, firm, convincing, and sufficiently grateful. I recall the following points in the letter I sent: I couldn't in all decency, I said, walk out of my job with the City after so short a period of employment (I had not then been in Saint John for a full year); I could not detect in myself any desire to get out of education and into journalism; I did not think, despite Mr. Robinson's flattering confidence in me, that I would make a good editor; and finally – and here I took the bull by the horns – I was convinced that sooner or later I should come into violent conflict on the editorial page with the political and economic views of both Robinson and Drummie. A few days after I had posted the letter, I met Howard Robinson in the lobby of the Admiral Beatty Hotel. He expressed his regret that I couldn't see my way to become his editor, and said – I particularly liked this – that I had lost nothing in his regard by my frankness.

The other incident was trivial and amusing and yet, in a way, no less astonishing. While I was at Mt. A. the CBC had sent a sort of talent-scout to the Maritimes. Charlie Krug, professor of philosophy, and I, professor of Eng. Lang. and Lit., were picked to do some radio broadcasts. I had given a series of "popular" talks on etymology and various language usages. The CBC asked me, when I was in Saint John, to do a couple of series of fifteen-minute book reviews, which with blazing originality I called "Books for the Times." Each series lasted for thirteen weeks. One day, after the series had been going for some time, I dropped into the Bank of Nova Scotia on Prince William St. to cash a small cheque. My bank was the Royal, but the cheque was drawn on the Nova Scotia. I was not known in the Bank and had nothing with me to serve as identification. I approached the teller, and offered the cheque. As soon as she had examined it she said "Oh, I'll cash this all right." When I had my money safely in my pocket I asked her why she was willing to cash the cheque. "I knew who you were as soon as I heard you speak," she said. "All I had to do was match the endorsement with the voice." A trivial incident, but consider its implications. My name, that of a young, hitherto unknown Maritimer, was becoming known across Canada, in some of the northern States, and even in Bermuda. I began to get letters from "fans" – old students of mine, a farmer's wife in Saskatchewan, a listener from a small Ontario town who disagreed with my derivation of a word, young people in Minnesota, a chap in Hamilton, Bermuda.... It was wonderful, and a little terrifying. I'm positive that one of the reasons that later I was asked to go out to Manitoba to talk about the university presidency was that these broadcasts had made my name known there, and had placed me, whether rightly or wrongly is not the point, in the category of scholar and critic, "presidential material." How utterly ridiculous when one thinks about it.

A school building burned down, and we had to get to work on plans and a contract for a new one. I found the burden of regular administrative work and school inspection impossible to carry without stumbling. There were between twenty-five and thirty schools in the city. After consultation with my chairman and one or two other Board members it was agreed that there was a clear case for the appointment of an Assistant Superintendent. I went over in my mind the list of School Principals, one of whom I thought should be the man for the job. I selected my man – and had my nomination turned down, and for a reason I had failed to anticipate. Among the schools under the control of the Board several were Roman Catholic. The Protestants and the Catholics got along beautifully. I inspected both groups, and was always received, everywhere, with courtesy and every sign of cooperation. The man I had nominated for the post of Assistant Superintendent was the Principal of one of the Protestant Schools. At that time I had not accustomed myself to thinking, when a job was to be filled, in terms of Protestant and Catholic, Gentile and Jew, French Canadian and English Canadian, Liberal and Conservative. I simply – and I mean simply – looked for the best qualified man or woman. But I learned! The Board itself blandly proposed for the job Lew McMurray, one of the Catholic Principals, and appointed him. Since I was a Protestant, it had been obvious to everyone but me that the new man must be a Catholic. I recognized my lapse for what it was, and awaited Lew's arrival in my office. He was an excellent man and proved well-suited to take over the new position. We became good friends and effective colleagues.

Between us we managed to get some good things done. Among them was the creation of modest school libraries. At that time, none of the schools, as I remember them, had any books on hand other than the texts prescribed by the Provincial Department of Education. We thought it worthwhile to suggest to the youth of Saint John that not all learning and wisdom and fun were to be found in the pages of their official readers, geographies, and histories. The Board managed to pry loose enough money from the City Fathers for us to make a start on this laudable enterprise, and we took a good deal of pleasure in distributing our purchases to the eager principals.

CHAPTER TEN

Early in 1945 I was asked by Judge Bergman, Chairman of the Board of Governors of the University of Manitoba, if I would care to come to Winnipeg to be interviewed and considered for the presidency of that institution. I was not completely surprised by his long-distance telephone call, since a Saint John friend, Tom Macnabb, General Superintendent of the CPR and a U. of M. graduate, had hinted to me that an approach might be made. Of course I went to Winnipeg. It was a journey that marked the beginning of the most difficult experience in my entire professional life. As I look back on it, I realize that I was something of an innocent when I walked into the presidential office. I had made almost no inquiries about the University. I knew little or nothing of its reputation, or of the local ground-rules under which it operated.

After a pleasant enough meeting with Judge Bergman and one or two other members of the Board, it was apparent that the offer would be made. Walter Crawford, the University Comptroller, drove me out to the Fort Garry site, about seven or eight miles away, for a look at the campus and to be generally informed. The Chairman had given me one clear warning, the significance of which I didn't grasp until somewhat later. He said, "I consider it very important that the new President get along well with Mr. Crawford." A question, immediately suppressed, popped into my mind: "That's odd! Doesn't he think it even more important that Mr. Crawford get along with the new President?" But I dismissed the reflection on the grounds, I suppose, that Mr. Crawford was no doubt an old and valued employee, perhaps a little crusty, but very efficient, extremely useful, a fixture in the place, and so forth.

Walter Crawford was indeed a valued employee, and most competent in the handling of the University plant and business affairs. He was also perhaps more than a little crusty: a plain, blunt man who had no use for tact and diplomacy. Sidney Smith, my predecessor, who had been made the President of the University of Toronto in 1944, once told me with great amusement, and as a little side-light on Walter's personality, that one day the Comptroller made a breezy entrance to the President's office, and said, as he flung down a few papers on the desk, "Here are the facts you wanted for those letters you're going to send out, Sid. You put in the bullshit."

I suppose Sid was right to find this harmless and amusing, but I, lacking Sid's knowledge of the place and his experience of Western informality, was inclined to query the implied relationship between the Comptroller and the President. If these manners and this personality had been the sole reason for Bergman's warning to me, all might have been well. But they were not the sole or important reason. I soon found out what I should have known from the very beginning, but had failed to discover: the Comptroller was separately responsible to the Board; not, that is, through the President. He was perfectly free and within his rights to go, without my knowledge, to the Premier, the Minister of Education, the Minister of Finance, and of course to the Chairman of the Board himself, to discuss University affairs. He was at liberty to express his own opinions – often, I'm sure, differing from mine – and to exert his not inconsiderable influence. And Crawford was not the man to refrain from the exercise of his rights and privileges. But he was capable. Within the area of what I considered his proper responsibilities, it would have been difficult to find a more competent man – admitting, however, that the roughness of his tongue, and his scorn of tact and diplomacy, left something to be desired.

It was now clear to me why the Chairman had emphasized that the President must get along well with the Comptroller. It's not too much to say that as far as the Provincial Government, and the business affairs and financial management of the University were concerned, the President played second fiddle to the Comptroller. It is true that almost any system of university government and organization can be made to work, after a fashion, if all the principal parties are men of good will and determined to make it successful. But Crawford had no genuine disposition to work closely and in harmony with the President, and I, I confess, found it difficult to endure the absurdity of the system and to make tactful and even obsequious advances to him. I believe, too, that I did rather less than I might have; used less patience and imagination than I might have; poured less oil than I might have (Sid Smith was much better at this than I was); and ran to the Chairman of the Board for consultation and guidance rather less frequently than I might have.

This form of government at the University of Manitoba had originated in the wake of an unhappy occurrence in the early thirties, when, under a loose and casual system of auditing, the Bursar had been able to embezzle large sums from the endowment fund. He was also the treasurer of the Diocesan funds, into which, too, he dipped heavily. The judge who had tried the case told me that for a time the Bursar had been able to switch securities from one fund to the other whenever he knew that an audit was coming, but that eventually there was not enough left in the two funds taken together to make up the sum of one. The poor fellow did not enrich himself at all; his "borrowings," as no doubt he regarded them, were used to meet obligations incurred in his shaky real estate business. The Provincial Government, once this situation was laid bare, decided to clean house. A new Board of Governors was appointed for the University, among its members being Walter Crawford. The new governors, quite naturally appalled by the events that had occasioned their appointment, were determined to run a tight ship. They asked Crawford to resign and take over the office of Comptroller, together with that of Secretary to the Board. And they made the Comptroller directly responsible to the Board, rather than through the President.

Under this arrangement, quite obviously an institution is split straight down the middle. One can understand the anxieties of the Board, this new broom for clean sweeping. But the circumstances, difficult though they no doubt were, obscured in the minds of the governors a fundamental principle of university government: the function of the governors and of the administration – Boards, Presidents, Comptrollers, Registrars, Deans of Faculties – is to create whenever necessary, to maintain at all times, and to improve whenever possible, the conditions under which the proper work of the university may best be carried out. That work is carried out by the various academic faculties and their students, not by the Board and the administration.

I don't want to be misunderstood. The dictum which I have rather pompously stated is not intended to be demeaning or a reduction in importance of the administrative and governing function. Obviously that function carries great consequence; it must be performed with skill and dedication. But the dictum must be understood and kept always in mind. The university teachers and researchers may not be regarded as employees of the Board. In a real sense, the administrators and governors are the servants of the teachers, researchers, and students. But I don't care to stress the servant relationship. It's no doubt a better notion that the two bodies constitute a unique type of partnership in our society; one that can be succcessful only if there is a complete understanding among its principal associates, a strong disposition to work in harmony, and a clear recognition that the functions of the one cannot be usefully considered in isolation from the functions of the other. The great fault of the Manitoba scheme, as I saw it, was that it provoked, constantly, a separation of the two basic functions; and since finances and campus business were inevitably closer to the Board and much more easily comprehended than academic affairs and the type of learning and thinking they involved, it tended to exalt the immediate and more readily comprehensible at the expense of the further removed and less easily understood.

I have already mentioned that the Comptroller was also the Secretary of the Board. I assume that the decision to entrust these two functions to the same man arose from the Board's early anxieties and its consequent determination to maintain the closest possible supervision of all affairs. In my opinion, however, this decision gave too much influence to one individual. It was bad enough to make the Comptroller independent of the President and directly responsible to the Board: to make the same man the recorder of all discussions and decisions, and the author of all Board correspondence, compounded the danger. He brought to the office of Secretary the authority and prestige inherent in the office of Comptroller; the greater office magnified the lesser. Everything in the way of Board record and communication was strained through the mind of the University's premier accountant and business man. Without blaming Mr. Crawford, who did what his nature and the rights and privileges of his two offices bade him do, I am convinced that the dual function tended, on the whole, to expedite business and finance, and to fall short of reflecting and meeting adequately, in all their variety, complexity and subtlety, the needs of academe.

The situation, as I saw it, urgently demanded participation by the faculties in the government of the University. I would have given anything to have a few of my professors sit with me on the Board. I saw two major reasons for such participation. In the first place, the President was, for the Board, the sole representative of the faculties; but he was an administrator, not a teaching, researching scholar. Complete responsibility lay on him for bringing academic needs and points of view to the attention of the Board, and for making the Board understand them. Under these circumstances, any conscientious President, having the necessary academic qualifications, interests and sympathies, is bound to be driven back, as it were, from the Board to the Faculties; he will become identified by the Board, and indeed I was so identified, as essentially a faculty man. To the faculties, however, he is an administrator and a Board member, and they can never be quite sure that he is representing them and their needs adequately or even honestly. Furthermore, they can never be certain that he is bringing back a full and fair account of Board reaction and opinion and policy. The members of the Board, on the other hand, tend to feel that the President, though a member *ex officio* of that august body, is not really one of them, or – since in fact he *is* a member by law – is one with an isolating difference. There are many worn but popular phrases which describe the President's position as I deeply felt it: I was between the devil and the deep blue sea; on the horns of a dilemma; falling between two stools; between the upper and the nether millstone.

No doubt other university presidents of my time would maintain that I have exaggerated the isolation of the president's position, they, too, having had no faculty representation on their boards. But I can tell the story only as I personally know it. The helpless discomfort of this standard situation was in my case aggravated, as I have been at some pains to make clear, by the unique authority and influence of the Comptroller-Secretary office.

My second reason for wanting faculty representation on the Board was that by no other means could I believe that the academics themselves would ever achieve their proper status in the eyes of the Governors, and take their proper and logical place in the determination and disposition of university affairs. This they would do simply by being members of the Board, and by demonstrating, directly, not only their needs and points of view, but their undoubted capacity to take an effective part in the discussion of all university affairs, academic and otherwise. In short, I came to believe then, and I have continued to believe, that a Board so constituted would greatly improve liaison and understanding between the Governors and the faculties, would provide a much more enlightened and effective means of deliberation on all the University's affairs, and would give professors and researchers their proper status in the eyes both of the Board and of the Provincial Government.

One evening, as the Chairman asked if there was any other business, I spoke up: "Mr. Chairman, I don't want to prolong this meeting, but I'd like to mention briefly one matter for later discussion and investigation. It seems to me that the grounds at the Fort Garry site are not adequately lighted at night. I often work in my office in the administration building until ten or eleven o'clock in the evening. I walk back to my house, at some distance, in almost complete darkness." I had this condition in mind because recently we had been having some breaking and entering and theft on the campus. To my surprise and dismay, the Chairman said, sharply and rudely, "Mr. President, you are out of order! All matters of this kind fall under the authority and responsibility of the Comptroller, and must be raised by him." Dead silence followed, which it was left to me to break: "I can't agree with you, Mr. Chairman." Then the meeting adjourned. Immediately afterwards, two members of the Board approached me; each of them said something about being sorry – I believe one of them said "indignant" – about the way the Chairman had treated me. I attempted to smile off the affront. What I might have said, but didn't, was "Then why the devil didn't you speak up and give me a hand?"

The status of the faculty member is only too clearly indicated by the following incident. One day I was meeting with the finance committee of the Board when the Comptroller proposed that the salary of the Assistant Comptroller be raised to X dollars. The Assistant Comptroller was a good man, and I could not object to the proposal that his salary be raised. But I felt I had to make the point that the figure named would place the Assistant Comptroller's salary above that of every member of the academic faculty, including the Deans, and that in my view this would be illogical, unfair, and therefore inexpedient. The Comptroller, without waiting for anyone else, broke in: "Good businessmen are hard to find; professors are a dime a dozen." This shocking remark was received without apparent resentment and certainly without rebuke by the Chairman (who was the Chairman of the Board) and by the other members of the committee. Three thoughts occur to me as I recall this contemptuous reference to the academic side of the University: first, the Comptroller would not have made it unless he had been perfectly sure that it was safe to do so; second, if there had been academic representation on the Board of Governors and on the finance committee, the remark would not and, I believe, could not have been made; third, and most important of all, if there had been such representation, the attitude so clearly betrayed by the remark, and accepted without demur by the Board members, could not have lived and flourished.

I could go on with story after story of unhappy situations that arose during those three years at the University of Manitoba. Some of them I handled satisfactorily; some of them I didn't. As I look back at this difficult experience, I'm happy to say that I'm not conscious of wanting to knife anyone. With Crawford I never had a quarrel. Judge Bergman was a logical man, with no suspicion that logic, like patriotism, is not always enough; he was without flexibility or much imagination, tough, and certainly devoted to the interests of the University as he conceived them.

With the faculties (except for Medicine) and the students I had excellent relations. Sid Smith had told me, on the eve of my departure for Manitoba, that he was sure I would like the young Westerners – informal, outspoken, and full of "git-up-and-go." He was right, although they got me, on one occasion, into deep trouble – though only briefly. A great deal of University instruction was carried on in the city itself, seven or eight miles away from the main Fort Garry campus, in a large temporary building situated on Broadway just across the street from the Legislative Building with the Golden Boy on top. Admittedly, conditions in the temporary buildings were not good. Everyone with whom I had talked, including the Chairman, told me that our location in the downtown building was temporary, and that the Board was anxious to consolidate instructional facilities on the Fort Garry campus as soon as possible.

During my early days in Winnipeg, I secured an appointment with the Premier, Stuart Garson, to make myself known to him and to have a general talk about University affairs. Just before I went to keep the appointment I learned, to my surprise, that a delegation of students had gone to the Premier to report conditions in the temporary building and to ask for improvements. Amused by this gutsy, young Western performance, I rather easily assumed that Garson, too, would be amused by its brashness, naïveté, and impropriety. When I walked into his office I said, by way of starting the conversation, "Well, Mr. Premier, I hear that you have had a visit from some of our students," and I'm sure I grinned as I said it. He replied, "Yes, I have. Sit down!" And then he rode me with spurs for eighteen minutes by my watch, obviously in a rage over the whole affair, and resentful of me for the part he assumed I had played in it.

The first time he stopped for breath I broke in to protest that the students had acted on their own volition and quite without my knowledge and consent. He refused to believe me. Thrusting across the desk the latest issue of *The Manitoban*, the student paper, he said, "Look at this!" There on the front page were two feature articles, one on the students' protest to the Premier about conditions in the temporary building, and one reporting an interview with me in which I was correctly quoted as having said, in response to a question, that I hoped we would soon be able to abandon the downtown temporary building and move to more satisfactory quarters on the Fort Garry campus. Because of the juxtaposition of the two articles, the Premier assumed that I and the students were in cahoots, and that I had inspired the delegation. He saw the arrival of this delegation, followed so promptly by my visit to his office, as a calculated criticism of the Government for not having provided the University with better temporary quarters, and as an attempt to whip up publicity and exert pressure on the Government to provide funds for more building at the Fort Garry site. When finally he stopped, I said: "Mr. Premier, I completely agree that it was quite improper of the students to come to you in this way and for this purpose. Obviously they should have come to me. I reiterate that I knew nothing about their visit to you. I learned of it only shortly before I came here. Mr. Premier, you *must* believe what I say." He looked at me for a moment, his anger having cooled, and said, "Of course I believe you, Mr. President." And after that I was on excellent terms with him. But what a hell of a way to begin my relations with the Government!

Sometimes the academic mind, painfully drawn towards one compelling goal, is capable of wonderfully incongruous behaviour. Shortly after the Fall term opened, in order to introduce and welcome new members of staff, we used to hold a general faculty meeting. Departmental heads would speak, each using much the same words: "I present Dr. Blank, who has recently completed a brilliant doctorate at Toronto – or Harvard, or Queen's, or wherever. He is a specialist in such-and-such a branch of his subject, and a distinguished addition to our ranks. I ask you to give him a cordial welcome to the University." On one occasion, after half an hour of such introductions, the head of one of the science departments rose to take his turn. What he said was laughable, and at the same time acutely embarrassing to everyone, not least to the young men he introduced: "I'm sorry to say that I can't make the kind of report that the other departmental heads have been making. I have been disappointed in my search for new staff; wholly unable to find first-rate men like those who have been – uh – secured by the others. Here is Mr. So-and-so, M.A. from the University of X. Here is Mr. So-and-so, M.A. from the University of Y." An incredible piece of gaucherie!

As I look back at all the difficulties I experienced at the University, it seems to me that the basic problem, considered quite apart from the personalities of all of us who were involved, was two-fold. First, the University was obstructed in its operation and development by an unrealistic system of government, which concentrated too much power in the hands of a few – and not always the best few – and admitted to the deliberations of the Board far too little academic expertise and influence. Second, the University was very young – I was only its fourth President; its origin was the College of Agriculture, and the agricultural interest, as represented on the Board, was so strong that sometimes it appeared to me that the tail wagged the dog. Out of this total situation there had not yet arisen a valid "idea of a university," in the Board, in the Government, in Winnipeg, and throughout the Province. To this may be added, as a natural consequence, that the University was not adequately financed; and that fact was necessarily reflected in the low salary scale, under-nourished research, low morale, and our great difficulty in engaging and keeping academic staff of high quality. Certainly we had many very able professors and a few flourishing departments, but the yearly turnover was much too high, and I found it almost impossible to persuade young and able scholars to join us. I recall talking with one such young man from one of the Eastern universities, to whom I had made an offer. He turned me down and said, "I might as well tell you that when I talked your offer over with the head of my department, he said 'If you want to leave us to improve your prospects, by all means do so. But don't go to Manitoba! Out there they'd steal the pennies off a dead man's eyes!'" I can't recall anything about my job that was more discouraging than the realization that the other major universities of Canada had such an unpleasant image of the University of Manitoba.

My principal reason for rehearsing these by now ancient matters, is to make clear what has not always been understood by the general public – the underlying reasons for the strong movement over the past twenty or twenty-five years to secure academic participation in the government of our universities. Admittedly, my stories of the bad old days are all taken from what was possibly the worst university situation in Canada at the time, as I was kindly told by several of my presidential colleagues, after I found myself up to my neck in it.

We've come a long way in the last few years. I confess that I have not always been completely happy about the ways in which university professors have discharged their new and important responsibilities; but on balance, there can be no doubt that the development of academic participation in university government was necessary and inevitable, and that it has brought about a considerable and desirable advance in that government in Canada.

I'd like to round out these Manitoba reminiscences with a humorous anecdote – one that, like so many of its kind, is something more than funny. A very good friend of mine, Bernard Naylor, an excellent English composer, came to Winnipeg as conductor of the Winnipeg Philharmonic Society while I was there. After several pleasant musical sessions at my home and his, Bernard asked me if I would sing two groups of songs at the next Philharmonic Society concert. Before agreeing to do so, I deemed it wise to test the water. I went to Bill Parker, member of the University Board of Governors and Chief Executive Officer of the Manitoba Pool Elevators, to discover whether he thought the Board would consider it objectionable if the President of the University were to appear in public as a concert recitalist. Bill was obviously uncomfortable, but he wasn't ingenious enough to produce a plausible reason for me to refuse Naylor's invitation. I sang, and, I'm thankful to say, had favourable criticism in the Winnipeg press. After I resigned, in 1948, the University had some difficulty in finding a successor, for, as the Chancellor told me in a burst of confidence over a drink, two or three tentative approaches by the Board had been firmly rejected. But one day Bill Parker stopped his car by Gertrude Laing's house – she later became Chairman of the Canada Council, and told me this story – walked over to where Gertrude was tending her flowers, and said, "Well, Gertrude, you'll be glad to know that at last we've found a new President for the University – and he doesn't sing!"

CHAPTER ELEVEN

Shortly before I became President of the University, I had been made a member of the CBC Board of Governors, of which Davidson Dunton was the recently appointed Chairman. My new duties at the University proved so heavy and so varied that I had to resign from the Board. I did so with great reluctance, not only because the experience of working with the CBC was exceptionally interesting, but because of my admiration for Davidson Dunton.

Dunton was an excellent Chairman. He quickly acquired the wide range of information needed, and he handled meetings quietly and firmly, with a quick and sensitive understanding of the mood and trend of the occasion. He was especially skilful in dealing with applicants for licences to operate new radio stations, as well as with those already licensed and making lots of money, who were trying to wangle ways of making more. His policies were sound. As an administrator, wise, firm, accommodating – I use the word in its proper sense, making firm and appropriate adaptation to circumstances – I believe he had few peers and no superiors.

When I asked Sid Smith who would be waiting for me in my office at the University of Manitoba, he blew a kiss to Heaven and replied, "The best secretary in the world, Gladys Yelland." In my three years at the University, I found every reason to agree with his high opinion. She was expert in every branch of her profession: highly intelligent, hard-working, accurate, cheerful, sympathetic, imaginative, and loyal.

After a year in office, I found desperate need for a second-in-command. It was proving impossible for me to confer as frequently and helpfully as was desirable with Deans of Faculty, Departmental Heads, Senior Professors, prospective and new members of the academic staff, heads of student organizations, and, of course, with

Board members and many, many others. I was somewhat reluctant to approach the Board with this problem: no one, including myself, was in favour of anything that might look like empire-building or bureaucratic proliferation. I softened my overture to the Governors by avoiding the term Vice-President, suggesting instead that it would be helpful to have a Dean of the University – a sort of Dean of Deans, in fact. I believe I got the idea for this office and its title from Harvard. To my surprise and great pleasure, the Board readily accepted my proposal. I at once asked Peter Armes, Dean of Science, to take the job: again to my great pleasure, though not to my surprise, he agreed. It was an enormous relief to have this wise, humane, and humorous man at my side.

One day in the spring of 1948, I answered a long-distance telephone call. The Premier of New Brunswick, J.B. McNair, was on the line. He said, "Don't you think it's about time you came back home where you belong? Milton Gregg has resigned from the presidency of UNB and we need a good man to take his place. I have been authorized by the Senate (the UNB name for the Board of Governors) to offer you the post at a salary of eight thousand dollars plus a free house and other small perquisites. I'll be frank, and tell you that I have been given a little leeway on the salary. Are you interested?" I wasted no time in saying I was, but I didn't drive a tough enough bargain. I said, "About the salary, Mr. Premier: what you're offering is exactly what I'm getting here. Could you put it up, say by five hundred? Just so that I can tell the Board of Governors that in addition to the other attractions of UNB and of going back to my old province, I am being given a larger salary?" He agreed, with what I should have spotted as suspicious alacrity. When I had a chance to look at the back minutes of the Senate I saw that J.B. had been authorized to offer me up to ten thousand. We came to terms, and I committed myself to take over at the University of New Brunswick on July 1, 1948.

John Macaulay, good friend, brilliant lawyer and a leader in his profession, was a bit angry with me. He and his group, he said, had stirred up a great interest in the presidential situation among certain well-disposed members of the Board and other influential citizens; if I had only held on for a few months longer, chances were, he thought, that almost everything I wanted would have been achieved: significant alteration in the form of university government, separation of the office of Comptroller from that of Secretary to the Board, direct responsibility, in the first instance, of the Comptroller to the President; improvement of the President's salary, and so on.

Well, perhaps!

In the summer of 1948 a Commonwealth University Conference was held in England – the first week in Bristol, the second in Oxford. I arranged with the University of New Brunswick to act as its representative at the Conference before taking office at Fredericton.

At Bristol, I found that most of us were assigned rooms in the university halls of residence. I very soon made the acquaintance of Jock Logan, later Sir Douglas, Principal of the University of London, and a good friend of the Halls. Ed Hall, President of the University of Western Ontario, and his wife, Lola Ruth, had chosen to put up at a Bristol hotel, where they had rather more elegant accommodations and rather more freedom of ingress and egress than we had at the University, as Jock and I were to find out. After the first day's business had been completed we went back to the hotel with Ed and Lola Ruth for drinks and talk – and all very jolly it was. It was well after midnight when Jock and I got back to our residence. The door was locked. No night porter was on duty. We knocked and banged and rang until the lady warden appeared in dressing gown, hair curlers, and a bad temper, to let us in. We had quite neglected to learn the local ground rules, but we knew them before we went to bed that night. We could scarcely blame the lady for her irritation, and we felt embarrassed and adolescent as we tiptoed past the rooms of the highly respectable, and dormant, Presidents, Principals, Rectors, *et al.* who had got in before curfew.

I don't remember much about the Bristol Conference. We sat and listened and talked, but no divine revelation of new truth was vouchsafed us. At least I don't recall any. But I do remember the welcoming banquet. Bristol had been terribly battered in the War, and the University buildings had not been spared. Consequently the banquet had to be given in a huge marquee. I recall with admiration the speech of the Vice-Chancellor, who made no reference to the devastations of the War, did not at all account for our being in a tent, and offered no apologies for the unconventional simplicity of the dining arrangements. "Up the British!" I thought to myself.

During the week, the University of Bristol held a special Convocation at which several eminent scholars and administrators were given honorary doctorates. The Chancellor, none other than Winston Churchill, arrived by car from London only just in time to don his robes and take the chair. It ws not one of his good days. We learned later that he'd had a rough time in the House the evening before. He sat sullenly, apparently paying no attention whatever to the eulogies delivered by the public orator, and he conferred the degrees, if not with reluctance, certainly with a minimum of grace. We were told that after the ceremony was over we might meet the Chancellor in an adjacent common room. Churchill appeared, walked across the room and sat down on a settee, at the furthest possible remove from a considerable gathering, and by his attitude dared anyone to disturb him. I thought to myself, "Damn it! I came in here to shake the great man's hand, and I'm going to do it." I separated myself from the party, stalked across the floor, stood before Winston Churchill, and said, "Mr. Chancellor, I have come to pay my respects. I'm Trueman of the University of New Brunswick," and put out my hand. He looked up slightly, gave me a limp handshake, said no word, and collapsed into himself again. I turned on my heel and rejoined my colleagues, some of whom were watching me, I gathered, with cynical amusement.

The most delightful and enduring of the friendships I made at the Conference in Oxford was with David Lindsay Keir, then the Vice-Chancellor of the Queen's University in Belfast, and his wife. He died a few years ago. David was a Scot, tall, dark, with a head that would have graced one of the great Roman Emperors. He was friendly, communicative, interested in things Canadian – his wife, Anna, is Canadian – a brilliant observer and analyst of the academic scene, with a delightful, dry sense of humour. Later, a year or more after we had established ourselves at UNB, David and Anna came over to attend a university conference at Dalhousie. I had been told of their arrival in Montreal by someone at McGill, who thought that the Keirs would enjoy having a look at the University of New Brunswick. With pleasant memories of my brief association with David during the Oxford Conference, I immediately sent word that we should be delighted to entertain them in the President's Lodgings for as long as they could manage to stay. We arranged that Jean and I would meet them at Harvey, a few miles up-river, thus saving them the inconvenience of travelling all the way to Fredericton Junction and transferring to our poky branch line, (now no longer in operation).

As we drove down the river to Fredericton we very soon got on friendly terms. I pulled off the road for a few minutes when Anna, who was in the back seat with Jean, told me what David himself had modestly held back: he had just become *Sir* David; and he had just been made the Master of Balliol, his old College. I still remember that when I looked at the new Knight in surprise and pleasure, he comically raised his arm before his face, as if in apology, or to ward off a blow that might be occasioned by this double presumption. Their visit with us was the happiest of events. I drove them to Halifax when Conference time came round. Unfortunately Jean couldn't get away.

The Halifax Conference, like most other academic conferences, pursued its languid way unmarked by anything in particular. But I have a story to tell of the last day. David and I had agreed that there was nothing in the final proceedings that deserved or commanded our interest. We decided that the three of us would drive down the South shore, past Chester and perhaps as far as Lunenburg, and picnic at some attractive spot on the way. We felt we should have something to drink with our lunch, but where and how to get it? (This was before the Enlightenment.) Just outside Halifax, we spied a man pushing a lawnmower in front of what appeared to be a small hotel. I pulled over and asked him if he could supply us. He said he couldn't, but if we'd drive along for a mile or so, partway round a curve to the left we would come to a small service station on the other side of the road; if we'd tell the man that Elmer had sent us, we might get something. It all turned out as he said: after a quick look at us which apparently quieted his misgivings, the man asked, simply, "Pints or quarts?" David said, "Quarts, by all means." So quarts it was. Our vendor warned us to get the stuff under cover quickly in case a prowling police-car came along. We headed back across the road to the car and Anna, Lady Keir. I shall never forget the sight of the Master of Balliol, with three or four big bottles cradled in his arms, looking anxiously up and down the highway, and then skipping nimbly across to safety. Shades of Jowett! If that isn't a new kind of Balliol story – and there are scores of Balliol stories – I'll never drink beer again. We drove on until we found a lovely field high above Lunenburg harbour and there we ate our box lunch and drank our warm, illegal beer in warm, sunny content.

After the Oxford Conference ended – we're back now in 1948 – I spent a week-end with Lord Beaverbrook at Cherkley. Then began five wonderful years at UNB, by no means free of problems, but all in all characterized by relations with the governing body and the financial administration that made the years at Manitoba appear by contrast like a bad dream. Of course, there was the Chancellor, Lord Beaverbrook.

I met Lord Beaverbrook for the first time at the Encaenia in May of 1948. When I was introduced to him he exclaimed "Why, this *is* a young man!" I didn't ask if he had been told I was young and had refused to believe it without ocular evidence. I suppose that from his point of view forty-six was young. I was to see him frequently enough during the next five years. As a matter of fact, the first serious business that confronted me at UNB was indirectly occasioned by Beaverbrook.

The Chancellor had indicated that he was prepared to build a rink for the University, a badly needed "facility," as we now say. It was rumoured that the site the Beaver had chosen was just inside the University grounds, next to the Beaverbrook Gymnasium. A group of Faculty members, and Joe Sears, the Bursar, got together to discuss what they considered a serious problem. The rumoured site was about as prominent as it could be. Rinks, they felt, were notoriously unlovely buildings. To place a rink right at the entrance to the beautiful hillside campus, at the end of University Avenue, would be an appalling aesthetic offence. The committee sent a letter to my predecessor, President Milton Gregg, stating their feelings very strongly, in language which could not be thought complimentary to Lord Beaverbrook's taste or judgment.

Somehow the letter got into the Beaver's hands. He was understandably angry. I arrived on campus and learned about it when J.B. McNair, the Premier of the Province, asked me to his office for consultation. The Premier wanted me to find out who had "leaked" the letter to the Chancellor. It had been sent to him anonymously. I didn't care much for this task, but I got the committee together and told them the story of the Beaver's wrath and the Premier's regret that anyone "up the Hill" should have been guilty of this act of mischief, which might well muddy the clear stream of his Lordship's benevolence. They all professed astonishment at the terms of the letter, which I gathered had been written by their secretary, Joe Sears. They couldn't imagine, they said, who had got hold of it and passed it along to the Beaver. I reported failure to the Premier and the matter was dropped, but festered for quite a spell, and the building of the rink was dropped for many years. Eventually the Beaver put one up, but not on campus.

The next problem that faced me was the urgent and immediate necessity of finding a Head for the Department of Mathematics. The man I selected and recommended was an Austrian, a fine scholar by the name of Rothenberg, to whom the University of New Brunswick must have seemed a strange institution indeed.

Rothenberg had a sense of humour, fortunately for him. His appointment at UNB was his first outside of Europe. I expected that he would find us and our ways very strange: our system of university government, our organization of the curriculum, our standards. And indeed he found it difficult to adjust his thinking and behaviour to the conditions he discovered in the department. The scholarly standards were low, and minimum demands were being made on the students; the small staff was accustomed to comfortable association with the head, and easy, informal consultation on all matters, great and small. I sensed that the department members were uneasy with this fine scholar of abstracted mien, who went earnestly about his researches, and failed to call his associates together for frequent consultation. I summoned him to my office and explained the ground rules hitherto observed in this small Canadian university, and advised him to call a meeting, and let his colleagues talk about the curriculum, examinations, tests, delinquent students, and so on.

A few days later he came back to report that he had held a departmental meeting. I exclaimed, with perhaps too much enthusiasm, "Oh, that's good!" "Vat's good about it?" was his sarcastic and disillusioned response. "I haff discovert dat de students don't know any mathematics whatsoeffer. Dey learned notting in high school, and ve haff not yet daught dem anyding here. But since I understand dere is in New Brunswick a law against bushing dem into de Saint John River, I haff decided to bass dem all and get rid of dem."

I suspect this solution of the problem was the only one possible from his point of view: a clearing of the decks, to be followed by more stringent demands of the next arrivals on campus, and an attempt to whip up more enthusiasm, throughout the department, for scholarship and research, accompanied by an appropriate staff recruiting policy. He made some progress: the department benefited from his work and example, but he did not remain for very long at UNB.

My relations with the Board started well and continued very well. (I'll call the governing body the Board, to avoid the confusion that might arise from the use of its actual name – a misnomer: the Senate.)

Lord Beaverbrook was the Chancellor for life. When I arrived, it was the custom for the Chancellor to take the Chair at meetings of the Board. This was to me a curious practice since by New Brunswick law, the president and Vice-Chancellor was ex-officio the Chairman. I never felt that it was wise for the President to have this double function, any more than I had thought it wise for the Comptroller at the U. of M. to be the Board's secretary.

At my first meeting Beaverbrook, with whom I had gone over the agenda, took the Chair and quickly began the proceedings. The first item of new business was my proposal as the new President that the inadequate budget for the Library be greatly increased – in fact, I believe, doubled. This suited the Beaver very well. He looked down the table with an intimidating eye, expressed his strong approval of my suggestion, and said, "I'm sure we are all in agreement? Passed!" It was the first time in my experience that I'd seen a "money bill" handled with such swift success. For a little while I thought that perhaps something might be said for having the powerful Chancellor act as Chairman of the Board. But I didn't hold that opinion for long: the chances were too great for equally swift defeat of something else that might be as dear to my heart as the improvement of the Library, but not of the same interest to the Chancellor.

The Board, taken as a whole, was an excellent assembly of able, concerned citizens. An old UNB friend of mine, who knew something about the U. of M., told me that I'd find my new Board a more aristocratic body than the one I'd known out West, and in a way he was right. It was a somewhat conservative Board, and it operated under a University Act that obviously needed many up-dating changes. To tell the truth, when we got round to the job of up-dating, we found it necessary to throw out most of the old Act and start almost from scratch. But the Board members, on the whole, knew what a university was all about. They understood what scholarship is, and the necessity and value of scholarly men to the university community. The Board didn't have anything like enough money at its disposal to do the job that was crying to be done. But its heart was in the right place, and no great issues of academic policy ever arose between us.

I tried to get the members to support changing their name from Senate to Board of Governors, but they were not at all moved by my appeal to general custom elsewhere. And after Lord Beaverbrook got tired of turning up at meetings to act as Chairman, and I took over, I tried to get them to let me off the hook, and appoint a Chairman from among themselves, if such an arrangement could legally be made. But they professed themselves happy with my officiating, and saw no difficulty in the continued union of the two offices. The difficulty that I saw was precisely the difficulty that I'd seen in another connection, at the U. of M.: the arrangement gave one man too much responsibility and too much authority and power. Although I envisaged no particular and immediate difficulty with the faculties, I thought it probable that sooner or later the familiar questions would arise, perhaps in aggravated form. At UNB, as at Manitoba and everywhere else, there was no academic representation on the Board of Governors. It's customary for any President to keep in close touch with the Chairman of his Board. But at UNB the President himself was the Chairman of the Board: not, I felt, a situation to be accepted forever by faculty members with quiet happiness, secure in a belief that the facts were always truthfully reported, their needs always adequately represented and explained, and Board decisions always clearly accounted for. It's not for me to claim a prescience exceeding that of my fellows in the profession; nevertheless, I must say I felt that old ways were beginning to be considered pretty seriously, and that challenging questions were soon going to be asked about representation, authority, and the modes of decision-making, and that better answers would be demanded.

Again I was lucky in my secretary. "Bing" Mackay was very efficient, energetic, fast-moving, agreeable and stoutly protective of my privacy. Her services were invaluable, especially during my early days; she was a UNB grad herself, and knew the campus personalities, the alumni and the alumnae, Fredericton society, and a great deal about the inner workings of the University.

The Bursar, as the chief business officer was called at UNB, was Joe Sears, a UNB and Oxford graduate – a Rhodes Scholar. He was legally trained and in fact gave law lectures on campus to pre-law or first-year students, who would later enroll at the Law School in Saint John. Joe, as a personality, was the direct opposite of Walter Crawford at the University of Manitoba. An easy-going, attractive man, never in a flap, not given to indignation, he was efficient in the discharge of the multifarious duties of his office, courteous, and on the whole tactful and diplomatic, except for his dealings with the Chancellor, which were, I'm afraid, anything but that. Joe broke me in.

One of the early matters I had to deal with was the academic record of the Beaverbrook Scholars. The Beaver maintained a number of scholarships for young New Brunswick students, at five hundred dollars a year, renewable for the four years of the undergraduate course. Five hundred was a sum, in 1948, that paid a considerable fraction of an undergraduate's annual expenses at UNB.

That summer of 1948 when I was in England, between leaving Manitoba and taking up my duties in Fredericton, I spent a weekend at the Beaver's magnificent estate at Cherkley. One morning he called me out to a balcony where he was taking the sun. He was in shorts, stripped to the waist, and wearing one of the broad-brimmed hats which he affected. He had before him a list of the UNB Beaverbrook Scholars, and a report on their standings for the last academic year, which he showed to me, expressing his great dissatisfaction with the average performance. It was not his intention, he pointed out, to provide scholarships for students who failed courses or made bare passes. Shocked by the record myself, I said "Leave it to me. I promise to change all this, and give you a much better report before the year is over." He grunted sceptically. "Do I have your authority to tell any delinquent who doesn't mend his ways that his scholarship will be discontinued?" He agreed heartily to that.

When term got going that fall, I called in the erring Scholars, one by one, reminded them of their low standings, and told them of the Chancellor's displeasure and of my assurance that the next report on the Scholars would be changed for the better – the much better. This was a situation which was academically intolerable, and clearly an occasion on which I could demonstrate to the Beaver that I meant business. Consequently I was pretty rough with these young people, and swore that I would strip them of their scholarships unless by Christmas they had given me unmistakeable evidence that they had settled down to hard work. After Christmas I was able to send the Beaver a carefully detailed report, in parallel columns, which showed, in every instance, an improvement in the standings. The report at the end of the year showed a very gratifying continued improvement. I sent if off triumphantly to the Chancellor, but I don't recall that I ever got more than a perfunctory acknowledgment of what had been accomplished. He wasn't inclined, I found out, to clap me on the back when I had done well for him, but he never failed to let me know when he thought I hadn't.

That weekend at Cherkley was memorable also for three little stories that are pure Beaverbrook. Perhaps I'm putting the memorabilia of two far-separated weekends together into one. No matter. One magnificent summer Sunday afternoon the house was filled with guests, and the Beaver had brought down from London a Yugoslavian dance group. We sat on the terrace looking out over a wide expanse of beautifully kept lawn. The dancers sauntered on to this green stage from right and left, as if out for a stroll. The two groups, in peasant costume, the girls in brightly coloured, swirling dirndls, met and mingled, chatted, and began to sing and dance. The setting, the costumes, the singing and the dancing were delightful. The Beaver sat motionless, hunched over, apparently in complete fascination. The house guests were to be given a late, deferred dinner in order that the dance company might first be properly feasted. As the performers' dinner ended, I looked in at the door of the dining-room, and heard the Beaver's little speech, which ran something like this: "You have given us a wonderful afternoon. I loved it all, especially the women, and to hell with the men!" Much applause.

At that dinner – or perhaps another one – the Beaver again made a little speech, in the course of which he lamented that his doctors had forbidden him to smoke, but he said, with the mischievous grin that has become celebrated, "I'm going to drink like hell!" At the same dinner he motioned to a servant to put a record on the machine in the corner. It was a wonderful, corny old song in which the rich man is admonished to mend his ways because all his silver and gold won't do him no good when the time come to meet his Maker. His pleasure in this song, in these surroundings, and as it obviously related to himself, was evident. Inspired by this amusing nonsense, he stood in his place and began to sing an old gospel hymn, "Shall we gather at the river...," "Will your anchor hold in the storms of life...," or some other specimen of the marine school of hymnology, I can't remember what. "Come on, Trueman," he urged. "Come on. Get up and sing!" I was damned if I was going to oblige him by taking part in this ridiculous performance, before a pretty fashionable group of people. "Come on, Trueman. Sing!" I said I didn't know the words – which was the truth. "Nonsense! Of course you know the words. Get up and sing!" I mastered my embarrassment and my anger – for I was indeed angry – sufficiently to rise in my place, but I reiterated that I didn't know the bloody words, and stubbornly refused even to hum the damned thing. I had a nasty feeling that I was being asked – no, ordered – to sing for my supper. At last he desisted and sat down. Oh well, I was young then, only forty-six! I suspect that if I could be in the same situation today, I would humour the old man, and – as he would say – to hell with the sophisticated English guests and their covert amusement at these philistine Canadian goings-on. Perhaps one can be *too* much on one's dignity.

One other story. We went for a walk, one day, through a long ride which had been cut in the forest land of the estate. The conversation fell on Lord Halifax, of whom I remarked that he ended every one of his speeches by some notably pious reflection or other. The Beaver snorted in derision, and said, "Yes! I don't think much of Halifax's piety and religion. For that matter, I don't think much of Christianity either." This by way of preface to an incident at dinner that evening. I recall having a meal – lunch I think – with the Beaver, alone, in the dining-room. My back was to a large French window which opened on a long walk, running beside a wing of the house. Beaverbrook said "Turn around, Trueman. Look out the window and along the path." I did so, and saw at the end of the walk and at the top of an easy rise, a large wooden cross, standing slightly askew. "What do you think of that?" By now I had learned that I must be careful not to lead with my chin, so I asked no questions but merely said "Very interesting. Very effective," and he let it go at that.

That evening, after our walk through the forest ride, there was a considerable company at dinner. On the Beaver's right was an attractive young woman, an actress I believe. I was on her right. We faced the French window. I heard the Beaver direct the young woman's attention, as he had mine, to the view of the path, with the cross at its end. She gave an exclamation of surprise, and said, "What's it there for?" And his Lordship replied with complete solemnity, "Symbol of my devotion to Christianity, my dear! Symbol of my devotion to Christianity!" What a mischievous, naughty old card he was!

CHAPTER TWELVE

As I have said, it was necessary to overhaul the University Act at UNB. I don't believe that anything had been done to it for half a century. It still contained a provision that the Chancellor, (the President), assemble the undergraduates every morning for the reading of scripture and a prayer. Pleasant as it was to be so reminded of ancient days, we obviously had to bring this piece of legislation up to date. Accordingly the Senate, that is, the Board of Governors, set up a committee. It consisted of Chief Justice Richards, Judge Peter Hughes, Joe Sears (the Bursar, who had legal training), and the President. We met for session after session in my office. There were literally scores of matters to be attended to. The principal one, in my opinion, was the creation of an academic senate; of course we couldn't call it that because our governing body insisted on retaining that title for itself. I suggested the name "Academic Council," which the committee adopted. It was a pleasant exercise to work out the details: the size of the body, the modes of faculty representation, the scope of its activities, the authority it should be given, and so on.

This was an interesting and revealing experience. I had never before taken part in the drafting of legislation. To state exactly what one means, no more and no less, and without ambiguity, is difficult enough under ordinary, everyday circumstances; but to accomplish the feat when one is putting a legal act together, is the devil and all of a task. I recall that after we had pored over a new section, or a new sub-section, perhaps for a couple of hours, and finally got it right, we would sometimes come back to our next meeting only to hear someone say "Do you realize that the section we drafted yesterday could be taken to mean something quite other than what we had in mind? For instance..." And so it would prove. No wonder lawyers can earn a living by finding loop-holes in the law.

Two little UNB stories will suggest just why I was so anxious to get a proper Senate created, and to have it recognized as the ultimate academic authority in the University. Despite my good relations with the governors and my respect for them as a more aristocratic and knowledgeable body than I had known at Manitoba, I have to admit that they showed something of the old, domineering, condescending – I won't say "Crawfordian" – attitude toward the faculties. At a general faculty meeting, the second or third year I was in Fredericton, a resolution was passed which in effect was a request that the faculties be allowed, once a year, to nominate to the governors appropriate persons for honorary degrees. Hitherto, the governors had prepared their own list on the recommendations of a committee made up of their own members. When the proposal came before the governors, the Chief Justice said, in surprise, "Why should the faculty be allowed to make recommendation to us for honorary degrees? After all, they are our employees!" My point is not the methods by which the recipients of honorary degrees should be selected, but the naïve assumption that the members of the Faculty work for the members of the Board of Governors.

The second story illustrates an even more heinous misconception and "malpractice." A certain student who had dropped out for a year or so came back and resumed his studies – speaking loosely. The quality of his work was indifferent and his attention to the details of the curriculum requirements, careless. At the end of his final year it was found that he had avoided taking one of the basic, required courses for the B.A. degree – it might have been Latin, or Math. At the last annual faculty meeting, when the standings of all senior students were reviewed, it was unanimously voted that this young man could not be graduated until he made up this deficiency. His indignant father went to various members of the governing body to protest against what he considered an injustice. When the faculty's list of graduands was presented to the governors, who by law were required to vote on it, someone referred to the omission of the young man's name, and moved that it be added to the list. The motion, after brief discussion, was passed, and the young man received his degree at convocation that week.

Deans and Professors came to me in fury. Apparently this was the first time that any of them had known the governors to exercise their powers in so arbitrary a manner. I thought I could see a little way into the future. I soothed my colleagues with "Don't worry! This is going to be all right. The governors' action is so preposterous that it will lead to a correction of the procedure." So it proved. Other parents whose sons and daughters had been held up because of a one-subject deficiency learned of the incident. And of course they said, "Is that all you have to do when your son fails by one subject? Go and squawk to a member of the Senate and get him to pull a few strings?" The governors soon felt the pressure, and in a chastened mood moved, seconded and passed unanimously a resolution that in the future no one could be graduated from the University of New Brunswick unless he had been recommended to the Board (the Senate) by the faculty.

CHAPTER THIRTEEN

In 1951, the Princess Elizabeth and Prince Philip came to the campus, near the end of a cross-Canada tour. The briefing that we'd been given prepared us for not more than a twenty-minute visit, but the royal couple stayed with us for nearly an hour. We received them on the Library steps, and took them into our "show" room, the recently completed Beaverbrook Wing, his latest gift to the University. We had provided a modest display of interesting books and documents, and one or two good portraits.

The Prince asked some questions about the rooms, which enabled me to tell him how the room came to be finished in bird's-eye maple. When we were preparing the specifications, we conventionally proposed Central or South American mahogany for the panelling and book-cases. Beaverbrook snorted in derision: in a province having an enormous forest area we ought surely to find something indigenous, he said, which would be beautiful and certainly more appropriate than mahogany. He was right, of course, and we settled for bird's-eye maple, although I'm sure I'm right in saying that it cost at least as much as the use of mahogany would have done. The contractor had to make a long search through the lumber yards of New Brunswick before he ran down a sufficient quantity of the stuff to do the job. This little story prompted the Prince to tell me that he and the Princess had received, as a wedding gift, a huge quantity of mahogany. What to do with it? "What can one do," he said, "with half a ton of mahogany?" I said, "Well, Sir, what in fact *did* you do with it?" He replied, "We had a few doors made up, and sold the rest!" I thought this an engaging "Mr. and Mrs." story, considering its source.

As soon as it became evident that the Princess and the Prince were not going to keep to schedule, one of the equerries proposed that tea might be served. We had made no preparation for refreshments and Heaven only knows how we scrambled a tea together. Of all the details of this impromptu operation I remember but one: the cups and saucers were thick, white, unlovely institutional ware, hastily pulled off the shelves of the library staff-room. But no one, including our royal guests, seemed to mind this. Finally the Prince asked, "Where are the students?" We were still standing about in the Beaverbrook Wing. I said that no doubt they were just outside, in great numbers; certainly too many to bring into the Library. "Then let's go out and see them," said the Prince. Out we went, Jean with the Prince, and I with the Princess. We walked about for several minutes, while the Princess and the Prince chatted with the students.

A story was told to me that evening about one of the Freshmen with whom the Princess stopped to chat. After she had moved along, his pals crowded about, with questions: "What did she say, Dave?" "What was she like?" "What did you think of her?" To the last question David answered simply "I'll die for her!" Shades of Anthony Hope! It was straight out of *The Prisoner of Zenda*.

My own most vivid memory of the afternoon was created when the Princess asked if the Latin motto over the Library entrance had anything to do with Lord Beaverbrook. Had he put it there? No, I told her. It was there long before the Beaver came around. The motto is *Ne me derelinquas, Domine*. Since I had no means of knowing if the Princess was a Latin scholar I tried as tactfully as I could to give the translation without seeming obvious and condescending. Well, having established the meaning as "Forsake me not, O Lord!," I told the Princess that a campus wag, mindful of Lord Beaverbrook's past generosity to UNB and hopeful of more, had provided a new and pertinent translation: "Forsake us not, Your Lordship!" She threw back her head and laughed. As soon as the royal visit was over, the newspapermen gathered around to ask what I had said that amused the Princess so much. I saw no reason for holding back the story, and it later got into the English papers, one of which was the Beaver's own *Daily Express*. I assume that his attention was directed to it, but he never mentioned it to me.

The royal visit was generally regarded as a great success. The Princess, though obviously tired from her long journey, was in a relaxed and informal mood, as was Prince Philip. But then, he always is, or seems to be. I was presented to him a couple of times in Ottawa, in later years, and as "Dr. Trueman." The last time – whether he recognized that I had been presented two or three times before, I can't say – he smiled amiably and asked a question, I forget how he put it, about my title. I stammered something to the effect that my doctorates – I was *gauche* enough to use the plural – were all honorary ones, and that I wasn't a doctor of anything in particular. He raised an eyebrow in mock astonishment, shot a mischievous look at me, and grinned. I moved along the line feeling a bit of a fool.

I had one flaming row with Beaverbrook. The background of the incident is interesting. Very near the end of an academic year I received a letter from Lady Dunn in which she asked that an honorary doctorate be conferred on Helen Mowatt, who had done some useful work down St. Andrews way in the encouragement of "arts and crafts." Sir James Dunn was either on our Board at the time, or had just resigned. I handed Lady Dunn's letter over to the honorary degrees committee. Their response was that they didn't think at all well of the nomination and that our list had already been made out: it was much too late to be considering other names. I was instructed to reply to Lady Dunn stressing the lateness of the date, the fact that our customary list had been completed for the year, and expressing our regrets that nothing could be done.

Now, this was the year in which the new Library Wing, the Chancellor's gift to UNB, was to be opened. Beaverbrook had arranged for a big "do" in the gymnasium, which we had to use as our auditorium, two days before Encaenia, and the day before the final Board meeting of the academic year. He had invited Dickie Law (Bonar Law's son), Lady Lloyd George, a newspaper tycoon from New York State, Frank Gannet, and other notables. After the Beaver arrived in Fredericton, a week or so before all this was to take place I went to see him late one afternoon in his suite at the Lord Beaverbrook Hotel. Fraser Winslow, the senior Fredericton lawyer, was present. As we discussed the arrangements, the Chancellor said, "I want all the students to be present at the ceremony." Since the show was taking place a couple of weeks after all classes had ended for the year, and a large percentage of the students would be scattered about the Maritimes, Quebec, and Ontario, already working at their summer jobs, I knew very well that the only undergraduates we could expect to attend would be the seniors, who were to receive their degrees. I said, "Well, Lord Beaverbrook, there's a difficulty about student attendance." He interrupted me with a snarl: "There's always a difficulty." Some cold words were exchanged, and then, obviously in an ugly mood, he mentioned Lady Dunn's request that the University give an honorary degree to Helen Mowatt.

"What's all this about refusing to give the honorary degree Lady Dunn asked for?" I gave the explanation. He snarled again: "I saw Jimmy Dunn in New York recently and he's furious. He says he'll never set foot on the UNB campus again." By this time I was beginning to get hot. Fraser Winslow was sitting there, listening to the Beaver give me the rough side of his tongue. I thought to myself, "Well, I can take only so much of this, and I've already had enough." I said, "We could scarcely anticipate that Sir James and Lady Dunn would take such an attitude, and may I say I think it's a hell of a poor attitude." He shouted "I think *your* attitude is a hell of a poor attitude!" He then flung himself back in his chair and said "I'm bored!"

By now I frankly didn't give a damn for anything, and I raised my voice to ask, "What are you bored with?" "I'm bored with you," he said. "You haven't put your back into this." By "this" I supposed he meant the arrangements for the opening of the Library Wing, student attendance, and perhaps the Dunn request. Without quite losing control, I slammed my folder of papers on the floor and said, "By God! this is too much. If that's the way you feel, after all I've done for you and for this University in the past three years, to hell with it! I'm getting out of here!" I scooped up my papers from the floor and walked out.

When I got home, I was still in a fury. Striding up and down the drawing-room, I told the story to Jean, informing her and the universe that I didn't need to be the President of UNB and if the price of being President was licking the Chancellor's boots, I wouldn't pay it. My wife had seen me in a rage before and, wise woman that she is, let me get it out of my system before she said, "You know, this is going to be all right. Calm down. Nothing bad is going to happen." Surely enough, within the hour the telephone rang. It was Albert, the Beaver's man-servant. He put his Lordship on the line. Abruptly, without reference to the scene in his suite that afternoon, he said, "I'm giving dinner here this evening. Will you and Mrs. Trueman come?" I said, very grandly, "Let me speak to my wife, to see if she is free." I cocked an eye at Jean and told her what was up. She nodded assent, and I told the old tyrant that we'd be there.

When we entered the suite at about eight o'clock I saw that Premier McNair, Dean Bailey of the University, and one or two others were present, including Mike Wardell, owner and publisher of the Fredericton *Gleaner*, President of the University Press of New Brunswick, and a member of the Beaverbrook stable. The Beaver promptly shoved glasses of whiskey into our hands and took the floor. He said, without any preliminary, "I made a fool of myself this afternoon. I quarrelled with the President over Sir James. And – saving your presence, Mrs. Trueman – I've never heard that bastard Jimmy Dunn say a sensible thing in all the years I've known him. I'm sorry!" I gulped and said something easy and brilliant like "Er-umph-ugh-glub," and took a long drink. From then on everything went with a bang.

The next morning I thought, "Well, damn it, the old boy really behaved handsomely. How many chaps in my position have had an apology from him, and before others too?" I sent him off a note in which I expressed my appreciation of his generous reference to our quarrel, and apologized for losing my temper, but carefully – I admit – avoided the issue that had provoked him and my outburst. As soon as he got the note, he telephoned me: "Have your note, Trueman. Quite unnecessary for you to apologize. The boot was on the other foot. Can you meet me in the Library at three this afternoon?" I met him at three. He said, "Now Trueman, I want you to know that I think you're doing a magnificent job as President. I'm a difficult man. I'm getting old and I have asthma, and people call me up on the telephone late at night from New York and London, and irritate me no end. If you can just remember this and make allowances, we can get along beautifully."

The ground was completely cut from under my feet. In an access of decent feeling and something much like remorse, I said, "My dear Lord Beaverbrook, I understand and appreciate what you have said. Believe me, anything I can do for you I shall be only too glad to do." And can you imagine what the old devil then said? He said "How about that degree for Helen Mowatt?" I stammered out a repetition of what the honorary degrees committee had decided, and suggested that although the matter had arisen too late for consideration this year, no doubt the committee would be glad to take it under advisement next year. He grunted, and we passed on to other matters.

But that was by no means the end of the affair. The big day arrived. Somewhat to my surprise, Sir James and Lady Dunn drove over from St. Andrews to attend the ceremony for the opening of the Library Wing. As we were struggling into our gowns and hoods, Lady Dunn

102

said "Oh Dr. Trueman, I've left my car in front of the building, where there is no parking. Will that be all right?" Sir James glanced at me and said sardonically to his wife: "Perhaps the President won't be willing to do that for *you*, Christofor." I promptly replied, with great enthusiasm, "Lady Dunn may leave her car wherever she likes," and if there was a suggestion in the tone I employed that I didn't care a damn what she did, I couldn't help it. After the ceremony was over, with peace at any price in my heart I approached Lady Dunn, whom we had placed in a special easy chair in the front row and expressed my pleasure that she had been able to attend the ceremony. She cut me short: "What about that honorary degree for Helen Mowatt?" Yet again I floundered my way through the explanation I had already given her and twice given to Lord Beaverbrook. She cut me short a second time: "It will have to be done on Thursday. She has already been informed."

I could only gawk at her in stupefaction. I assume that after our meeting in the Library, Beaverbrook had telephoned the Dunns in St. Andrews and told them that he'd handled the President, taken the starch out of him, and that when they came over for the big meeting on Tuesday, Lady Dunn ought to tell Trueman that Helen's degree must be conferred on Thursday, since she had already been told that it would be. The only comfort I can take out of this preposterous situation is that the Beaver had thought it worthwhile to go to the trouble of "handling" me. He might well have issued an order for me to convey to the governors. But obviously it was better from his point of view to placate the President and put him in a position which would almost certainly force him to give the desired recommendation to the Board. Cunning!

The next day the Board (that is, the Senate) met, and I told my story. The Beaver was not present. I said in conclusion that we could either refuse to grant the degree, or in consideration of all that Lord Beaverbrook had done for the University, and of all he might do in future, we could bite on the bullet and endure our pain. On balance, I suggested, we had better make the latter response. The Chief Justice spoke up, expressing his deep sense of shock, but agreeing that it would be wise, all things considered, to surrender. Judge Hughes, also deeply shocked, agreed with the Chief Justice and the President. In short, we consented to confer the degree the next day.

After the Board meeting I got on the telephone to Miss Mowatt and told her the glad news, and apologized for the delay in getting in touch with her, occasioned by one of those administrative kafuffles of which no doubt she'd had experience. Her reply was, "Oh, Dr. Trueman, what a lovely surprise!" The incident was closed off for me when at Encaenia next day I heard the Beaver, who was hooding the honorary doctors, murmur in her ear, "Duck your head, Helen, so I can put this thing on you."

I suppose it would be difficult to find a more disgraceful affair in the history of Canadian universities. The freedom of the University to make its own decision had been swept aside by the power of wealth, of position, of prestige. In all fairness it must be admitted that the Dunns had no notion of what a university is about and could not really comprehend the cherished fundamentals of its existence and its purposes. They are to be criticized for having made little or no effort to understand. But what rankled in my soul was the revelation that in the minds of these people, Beaverbrook included, I and my colleagues were regarded as properties to be moved about, whose sole obligation was to say "Yes, Sir. Certainly, Sir. As you wish, Sir." Our convictions, our feelings, our status were beneath notice. Perhaps I exaggerate here, but not by very much.

Beaverbrook was a complex personality. He could be ruthless and he could be merciful. He could be indifferent to appeals for help, and he could perform unexpected acts of great generosity. He could be intolerant and he could be gracious and understanding. He was sensitive to beauty in many forms. One thing he could not do: he could not provide money for, say, a building and then step aside and let the beneficiaries of his generosity get on with the job of planning. I've recorded his wise interference with our proposal to use mahogany for the finish of the Library Wing. He by no means stopped there. He required me to give him a list of the books that we wanted for the open shelves of his new and lovely room. And he examined the list, item by item. I can recall only two of the rejections that he made, although there were others. He absolutely refused to have the morals of young New Brunswick students corrupted by the poetic works of John Wilmot, Earl of Rochester. "No, Trueman. We won't have that in the Library!" He also deleted a book by Earl Browder, the American communist. He said he didn't object to it because it was written by a communist, but because Browder, in his opinion, was a damned fool. I was inclined to agree with this view of Browder, but not with the decision to keep the book out of the Library.

The ruthless way in which the Mowatt honorary degree was

forced upon the University was unforgiveable but, as we saw it, just barely endurable. Direct interference, however, in our academic courses would have been the last straw. We could not have put up with that. I confess that I fully expected the Chancellor to make at least strong and disapproving hints about our teaching of economics and history. But I heard nothing from him about any inadequacies or wrong-headedness in our treatment of free enterprise or of the nature and role of the Empire, now being called the Commonwealth. He scrupulously kept his hands off these issues. But he blazed out unexpectedly from time to time. He secured the R.B. Bennett papers and deposited them in the UNB Library. He thought it a good idea to have someone go quickly through them, find out in general what the material was, and make a preliminary classification. We handed the job over to a bright young man on our library staff, who got briskly to work, and sent progress reports, from time to time, to Beaverbrook. Unhappily, the young man thought he found something in the correspondence about certain land deals in the West which reflected disastrously on Bennett's character. The Beaver was furious that this young pup should dare to imply that anything could have been doubtful about the behaviour of Bennett, a great Canadian, who had been his old and close friend. I do not think that he actually called on us to get rid of the young man, but he came close to it.

Difficult as it was to endure the Mowatt incident, I didn't want the credit or, depending upon the point of view, the discredit, of being the man who separated the University from Beaverbrook and his wealth. As long as he did not interfere with our teaching of economics, political science, and history, I felt that we could put up with a good deal. It can't be denied that he was of great help to UNB, with his buildings and his scholarships. I think I was right to take this attitude, although I confess that after the honorary degree for Helen Mowatt had been set up by the Beaver and the Dunns, I wondered if I should not have urged the Senate to refuse the order, fight, and take the consequences. But, looking back over thirty years, I now have no regrets that I kept my temper and gave the advice I did.

The only other personal difficulty that arose in my time concerned Joe Sears, the Bursar. I'm sure that Joe didn't like Beaverbrook from the start, and resented the influence he wielded and the tone of authority with which he spoke. Joe was not the only one by any means to dislike this being moved-in-upon from the outside by a wealthy, powerful non-university man of world-wide reputation. To those members of the faculty it no doubt appeared that UNB had been taken over, if not wholly, yet in observable and objectionable measure. Just how the bad feeling began I do not know: I was not long on the campus before I realized its existence.

The pot boiled over when Joe sent Beaverbrook a wholly formal and curt note informing him that he owed "petty cash" a few dollars. The Beaver, I gathered, didn't often carry cash in his pockets; by arrangement, small sums were advanced to him as he needed them, on the understanding that the Bursar's office would keep track of these little loans, and from time to time give the Chancellor a statement of his indebtedness. I wasn't aware that this was going on. I must say that I think it was a bad arrangement, and I'm sure Joe thought so too. Chancellors shouldn't be making use of the petty-cash drawer in the University's business office. The practice makes unpleasant misunderstandings possible, even probable – as it clearly did in this instance – and calls for the exercise of tact, a quality which is not always in good supply, I have found, in book-keeping offices.

I can't quote the letter exactly, of course, and I shall not try. One day the Beaver threw it down in front of me, obviously angered, and said, "That's no way to address me! That's no way to write to the Chancellor of the University!" As I looked it over I had to agree that Joe had been seriously at fault in the form and style of his message. It was curt and cold. I seem to recall that after the Beaver's name and title, the body of the letter was introduced by "Sir," or perhaps it was "Dear Sir." A bare statement of the amount owing was made, and while I can't believe that a remittance was asked for in so many words, the thing undoubtedly sounded like a dun, provoked by unreasonable delay of payment – all this directed to a man who had given the University hundreds and hundreds of thousands of dollars in buildings and scholarships.

Almost immediately, I was called to the Premier's office to meet with him and the Chancellor. It became at once apparent that the Sears affair was to be the subject of our conversation. And it also became apparent that the Beaver had had it, and was not prepared to continue his interest in the place if it was going to be necessary for him to have financial, or indeed any other dealings with Sears. The Premier backed the Chancellor.

My heart sank. It was to me unthinkable that we should fire Joe. He was a UNB graduate, a Rhodes Scholar, with a brilliant record, and had been on our staff for years. He was well-liked and respected not only at the University, but in the larger community of Fredericton. But I could see no way in which he could continue in the Bursarship unless the University was prepared to do battle and run the very evident risk of losing Beaverbrook as Chancellor and benefactor. I felt sure that such a course of action would be widely condemned. However, I thought I saw a way out of the mess, if I could secure the approval of the two powerful gentlemen who confronted me, and the agreement of Joe.

As I have said, Joe's Oxford training was in Law, and on the Fredericton campus he gave lectures to pre-law or first-year law students, who later enrolled in our Law School in Saint John. I stated as boldly as I could to the Premier and the Chancellor, that I could not countenance Joe's dismissal from the University's employ. I proposed that he be asked to relinquish the office of Bursar, and accept a professorship of Law, with no reduction of salary, and with assurance that salary increases and pension arrangements would continue as before. I felt sure that if Joe would accept this proposal, we could work out a full-time schedule of instruction, with the cooperation of the School in Saint John. I was told to go ahead.

It was not easy to put this before Joe. Fortunately, he and I were on very good terms. He asked for a day or so to consider the proposed arrangement, came back when he said he would, and accepted. I consider that his behaviour was highly intelligent, cooperative, and magnanimous. He must have been boiling inside. And so we made him the Professor of Law on the Fredericton campus of UNB. He continued in the post for several years. We gave the Bursarship to an excellent man, another UNB graduate, Bev MacAulay, who eventually became the Vice-President, Administration, and a very good one, too.

Someone once asked me, "How did you 'handle' Beaverbrook?" My answer was, "You don't handle a great natural force, like a tornado or an earthquake, or a tidal wave. You survive – if you can."

One of his techniques was to keep his working associates off-balance. I had many conversations with him about the future of UNB and about immediate schemes for one purpose or another. But he seldom fully opened his mind. I never was certain that he had committed himself to precisely this or precisely that, or that he was enthusiastic about getting some new and specific thing done. One outcome of this practice was made clear to me by Jack McNair, the Premier. He told me, one day, that the Beaver complained that he couldn't get the cooperation he wanted from the University in the prosecution of his benevolent plans. And then on another day, Jack told me that the Beaver was unhappy because we were everlastingly pestering him to do this or that, and to provide the necessary money. In other words, if you were uncertain what the old boy wanted, and cautiously held back lest you jump the gun, he complained of lack of cooperation. On the other hand, if you moved quickly into some scheme he'd broached with you, you were apt to hear that he felt he was being unduly pushed and prodded. This may have been a protective device naturally developed by a very rich man whose money so many people wanted to help him spend. Or he may have thought that keeping people uneasy and uncertain of his intentions was a good way of assuring enthusiastic cooperation after he'd made up his mind what he wanted and could give clear directions. Or, it may have been, in part, a manifestation of the love of mischief which, as many writers have insisted, was an important facet of his many-sided personality.

No one could associate with him for very long without being convinced that he was a tremendously forceful man of considerable intellect. I can recall no one else who gave me such a strong conviction that I was up against raw power. I tried, more than once, to account for his great success in terms of what I knew of him. Granted the force of his personality and granted his first-rate mind, my conclusion was that the "extra" quality was tenacity of purpose and the ability to maintain concentrated interest in a cause, an issue, a problem; to continue to burn at white heat long after lesser men had lost their first ardour or accepted rebuff. I confess that after I had put in – say – ten to twelve hours of hard work on University affairs I was often tempted to say "To the devil with this! Let it wait until tomorrow. I've worked enough for today. I'm going to listen to some music, or finish that book I started." Not so the Beaver. I've been called to his suite in the hotel at ten in the evening and found him, after a long and busy day, just as vigorous, just as keen – and certainly every bit as difficult – as he had been at eight-thirty that morning.

He had moments of deep aesthetic emotion. I'm sure of that. I recall entering his hotel suite to keep an appointment, and finding him at the window gazing down at the Saint John River. Without turning away, he said in a low voice "My God, Trueman, it's beautiful!" I could see no reason why he should "act" before me. My memory goes back to that Sunday afternoon at Cherkley, when he seemed caught up in the loveliness of the scene and in the music and dancing of the Yugoslavian company. I never had any reason to doubt that he was genuinely moved by many forms of beauty. And the man did an enormous amount of good in New Brunswick. Of that there can be no question. I think I'm right in stating that before he died he had given away a considerable portion of his wealth and had secured, wisely and naturally, the proper distribution of what remained after his death.

I disagree strongly with the view that Beaverbrook was an evil man. I believe I have known only a very few evil men, very few indeed. And I certainly would not number Beaverbrook among them. It seems to me that there was much more good than evil in his nature and behaviour; and not much more than that can be said for the best of men. It is true that his conduct now and then led me to think of the difficulties rich men are said to have in getting into the Kingdom of Heaven and camels in passing through the eyes of needles. Perhaps I'm getting a bit soft as the years overtake me, although I find myself being irascible and condemnatory to a degree that I had always supposed foreign to my nature. But still I can applaud Dr. Johnson's sentiments. Boswell records these words: "I sometimes say more than I mean in jest; and people are apt to believe me serious: however, I am more candid than I was when I was younger. As I know more of mankind I expect less of them, and am ready now to call a man a *good man*, upon easier terms than I was formerly." As I look back to those days of association with the Beaver I am aware of curiously mingled emotions: anger, wounded pride – but that's not important – resentment, gratitude, amusement and – yes – affection.

CHAPTER FOURTEEN

It was during my UNB days that I was appointed a member of the National Film Board of Canada. What a fascinating experience that was! Arthur Irwin was the Chairman and Government Film Commissioner. The association with him and his wife, the poet P.K. Page, was stimulating and delightful, as was the relationship with the other members of the Board at that time, and with the film-makers themselves – Norman McLaren, Guy Glover, Don Mulholland, Bob Anderson, Nick Balla, Tom Daly and many others.

This appointment was to have far-reaching consequences for me, when in 1952 the government of the Province changed from Liberal to Conservative, with Hugh John Flemming as the new Premier. Politics is a grim business everywhere, but nowhere more so than in the Maritimes.

Since I had been appointed to UNB by a Liberal government the new regime assumed without reflection that I was a Liberal, despite the fact that the Truemans (my father, uncles, and grandfather) had always been Tories, and that I had never taken part in politics in any way whatsoever. As a matter of fact I was neither a Liberal or a Conservative, contrary to the political philosophy of the Sentry in *Iolanthe*. I was nothing, politically speaking. At this moment the University was in great need of a new Chemistry building. With Premier Jack McNair's promise of support I had gone to Toronto to talk with architects. Plans for the building had begun to go forward.

At my first interview with Hugh John Flemming I was informed – pleasantly, I must say, and with regret, but firmly – that the new government would not, certainly at that time, let us continue with the building. That was that. And when I let it be known that the University would soon present a budget for the coming year, a budget somewhat larger than the current one, Mac MacDermott, Provincial Superintendent of Education, told me that he had been instructed by his new Minister, a Mount Allison graduate, to inform me that no increase in the University budget would be granted at that time or in the foreseeable future. I never had a letter from the Minister or even a moment's conversation with him on this issue.

It seemed to me that my days of usefulness at UNB were drawing to a close. With the new government's determination to question almost everything that had been done or was about to be done by the Liberals, and my being tagged as "one of the gang" that had just been ousted, the future looked bleak. I reflected, too, that I could afford to have one row, and only one, with our powerful Chancellor, and I'd already had it. Even though I, personally, had emerged from the row unscathed, I couldn't see that a repetition of that kind of clash - and a repetition was bound to occur - could have anything but bad consequences for the University, and for me.

Then, one day in the late winter of 1953, the long-distance telephone rang again. On the line was the Hon. Robert Winters, the Minister (I forget what his portfolio was at the time) to whom the Film Board reported. Bob was a Mount Allison grad; in fact he had been a student when I was a young Assistant Professor in the English Department. I knew him well, and his brother and sister and cousin, all from Lunenburg, Nova Scotia. Without beating about the bush, Bob informed me that Art Irwin had resigned from the Film Board, and in accordance with an agreement he had made with the Government before he set foot in Ottawa, had gone into the diplomatic service; early in the summer he would be off to Australia as Canadian High Commissioner. Bob said, "How about coming to Ottawa and taking over as Chairman of the National Film Board?" I was surprised and, I admit, excited. From my point of view, the timing of the offer couldn't have been better. I told him that I was deeply interested in the Board, but attractive though his proposal was, I couldn't say, right then and there, that I was prepared to spend the rest of my years in that particular niche. "Don't worry about that," Bob said. "The Government is always looking for men qualified to fill high positions. Come and give us a reasonable period of service. Something else that will attract you is bound to come up." He gave me a few days to think it over.

Now just at that time, Dr. C.J. Mackenzie, President of the National Research Council, was on campus. While I didn't know Dr. Mackenzie personally, I knew him by reputation; that is to say I knew of him most favourably. We met the next day at a cocktail party. Realizing that one or two modest parallels could be drawn between the type of position he held and the one that I was being asked to take, it occurred to me that it might be useful to have a talk with him. On impulse, I asked for a few minutes of his time, and drew him aside into a vacant room. He was interested and helpful. He first said what any intelligent man is bound to say under the circumstances: whether or not to take the job was a highly personal matter for me, and me alone. He knew I didn't want him to come out with a flat-footed "Yes" or "No." But it seemed to him a good thing for government to seek out men who had been succcessful in the academic administrative world, and draw them into the public service. Such men often bring with them, he thought, a type of mind and of experience of great value in public, non-political positions. He, personally, he said, liked to see academics take up this sort of challenge; it seemed to him of value both to the university world itself, and to the public service. Later, as I recalled our conversation, I thought that what he said showed insight and made good sound sense. Still later on, I discovered that everything Jack Mackenzie says makes good, sound sense. I telephoned Bob Winters and told him I would accept the job, and not long after, I received official confirmation of the appointment, which was to date from July 1, 1953.

Between the date on which Art Irwin left the Film Board and the formal beginning of my appointment there was a gap of several weeks. The Board was thus left without a Chairman – its administrative head and chief executive officer – for a longish period. In late May I got a telephone call from Donald Mulholland, the Director of Production. An exciting thing was going on in Stratford, Ontario, he told me: the creation of a Shakespearean Theatre. The little community, to a man, had contributed money for the venture. Tyrone Guthrie had been secured as the first director, and no less an actor than Alec Guinness had promised to take the leading role in *Richard III*. Don felt that the National Film Board would be scandalously remiss if it didn't send a crew to Stratford at once, and get on with the making of what might well be a major film. He asked me for authority to set up the assignment and spend the necessary money. I told him that unfortunately I had no such authority, since I wouldn't become Chairman of the Board and Government Film Commissioner until July 1.

What to do? I was convinced that Don was right: the film ought to be made. I took a chance and told him to go ahead; if, later, he and his crew were criticized or even challenged for committing the Board to such a large expenditure, without proper authority, I would take the blame and fight any battle that might have to be fought. Away they went. Many months later, I named the finished product myself, not very imaginatively, "The Stratford Adventure." It turned out to be one of the best films the Board had ever made, and gained a distribution in Canadian theatres that broke all our records. So my first business with the National Film Board was conducted before I left Fredericton, and certainly before I had any legal right to conduct any business at all. And we never had any trouble about the question of authority.

One curious little memory comes to mind. We tried, without success, to get our crew inside the tent-theatre, to film Guinness in rehearsal; however, his agent in London claimed that the terms of agreement with the actor did not permit him to be filmed in these circumstances. We were able to "shoot" him riding a bicycle through the streets of Stratford and talking with a young aspiring actor, but we had to do without what would have been a most interesting and valuable record of him at work. A great pity. A year or so later, attending the Edinburgh Festival, one evening at the theatre I sat beside an attractive woman with whom I got into conversation. I introduced myself, and she told me who she was. And she was the agent who had refused to let Alec Guinness perform before our cameras on stage at Stratford. I forgave her, and dined her, and she became one of my good English friends – although I have long since lost track of her, I'm sorry to say.

During my first week officially in office I was given the unhappy news that in a recent cabinet shuffle Bob Winters had been moved to Public Works, and would not be my Minister. I went to see him as soon as possible. There, behind his desk, sat handsome Bob, grinning his white-toothed grin and enjoying the discomfiture his move had occasioned me. I cursed him, genially I believe, and he roared with laughter. He assured me, however, that my new Minister, Walter Harris, was an excellent man; able and likeable.

To be on the national scene in Ottawa was an exciting prospect. I had none of that provincial spite that exercises itself in constant disparagement of the Capital. I get heartily sick of those smart articles in our national press that take cheap shots at Ottawa, the city of civil servants, of bureaucracy, dull, uninteresting. I have not found Ottawa like that at all, and nor have thousands and thousands of sensitive and intelligent people who live there.

But it was not at all pleasant to pull up stakes and leave Fredericton. We had greatly enjoyed life at the University, and had made many friends whom we knew we should miss but inevitably lose touch with. Our hearts had gone out to the lovely surrounding country, dominated by one of the world's great and beautiful rivers, the Saint John. Jean and I still vividly recall our first drive along the winding roads of the neighbourhood – the old covered bridges, the wooded hills, the brilliant autumn foliage, all in delightful contrast with the prairies, where a Sunday afternoon drive consisted in following a straight line out of the city and making three right-angle turns; sensing nothing much more than flat distance and the vast, over-arching sky. Maritimers as we both are, we were caught too late for response to the beauties which native Westerners no doubt find, and rightly acclaim, in their level surroundings.

For the sixth time, it was necessary to move our household goods, the accumulation of twenty-two years of married life. For the sixth time for Peter, the fifth time for Sally, a change of school was being forced on them. Peter, now about to begin his third year in Arts at UNB, elected to come to Ottawa and register at Carleton, where in accord with an academic policy which I think unjustified he was made to do certain first- and second-year subjects not required in the UNB curriculum. Why hold up a young man for a year, or perhaps two? Two successful years in Arts at one respectable Canadian university ought to be thought equivalent to two successful years in Arts at another respectable Canadian university. Sally, with no choice whatever in the situation, had to come along, for disposal as her parents saw fit. Happily we were able to enter her in Elmwood School for girls, where she settled in with no major difficulties.

We found a place to live through the good offices of our old friend Freddie Johns, now Air Vice-Marshal Johns, stationed in Ottawa, who telephoned us in Fredericton with the information that houses were hard to find in Rockcliffe, where we wanted to set up our new home. Fred advised us to take at once a small house of many rooms on Minto Place. We commissioned him to rent it for us without our having set eyes on the place. It was a tight fit but otherwise attractive, and conveniently located for all of us.

My first real problem presented itself immediately. The Government had decided to move the NFB to Montreal, although the Chairman was to keep his head office in Ottawa, and the Still-Photograph Division was to remain in new quarters in Ottawa, along with some other administrative functionaries. My predecessor, Art Irwin, had been under the impression that all initial internal opposition to the move had been overcome, and that there was general agreement to the change, and even enthusiasm for it. This proved to be a mistaken view. Donald Mulholland – representing, as I soon discovered, most of the senior production staff – came to me with the news that the move was "viewed with alarm," and considered unwise and impractical. He asked if he might present me with a brief which would state the position in some detail, as he and his colleagues saw it, and if I would see that it got into the Minister's hands. Green though I was in dealing with the federal government, I could see at once that the situation was tricky. If I passed Mulholland's brief along to the Minister, no matter how earnestly I might try to dissociate myself from it, I would no doubt be seen as bucking the government's policy and decision: after only a few weeks in office, causing trouble, being difficult. On the other hand, I couldn't see myself suppressing opinion, denying my staff's right to make their views known to me, and to those with the power to reconsider the move and possibly to cancel it. I promised Don that I would study his brief carefully, and that I would see that it was put on the Minister's desk, with an explanatory note from me.

Harris took the thing home with him for a weekend. On the Monday he summoned me to his office. He was much impressed by Mulholland's arguments, and with obvious relish for the irony of the situation, informed me that he himself was the only member of Cabinet to express to the Prime Minister serious doubts about the wisdom of moving the Board to Montreal. He assured me that he thought Mr. St. Laurent ought to see the document at once, and that he was going to make sure that he did.

In a day or so I got a telephone call, not from my Minister, Walter Harris, but from Bob Winters, now moved over to Public Works. I went to see him at once. As I had expected, the Prime Minister had asked if the new Chairman of NFB was out to cause trouble. Why, after the move had been agreed to by all parties, was Trueman opening up the matter again? Was he likely to be difficult? While I was glad enough to talk with Bob Winters, I couldn't help feeling that the Prime Minister should have made his enquiry from Harris, the Film Board's Minister: perhaps he thought that Bob, who no doubt had proposed me for the Chairmanship, and was an old friend, would know more about me and could find out what I was up to more quickly than Harris. No doubt the Prime Minister communicated with Harris only after he got Bob's report.

I had no trouble in making Bob understand the logic of my action. I pointed out that I couldn't afford, in my very early days as Chairman, to antagonize my principal associates by refusing to listen to their opinions and refusing to inform the Minister that serious objections were being raised, internally, to the migration to Montreal. I also said that I would be doing less than my duty if I concealed from the Minister a situation of which he as yet had no knowledge, and which might develop into something serious if it were not handled frankly and honestly. Bob said, "Well, then, you are not heading up a revolt against the Cabinet's decision?" I said, "Certainly not. As I have explained, it seemed necessary for me to let my Minister know what's going on in the organization for which he speaks in Parliament. I've done my duty, as I see it, to my colleagues and to Mr. Harris. Now, if the Prime Minister feels that the matter has been settled and it would be pointless to raise it again, that's fine with me. I'll get on with plans for the new building in Montreal and for moving the staff and their families out of Ottawa, with all possible expedition." Bob said, "That's great! That's all Mr. St. Laurent wanted to know, and all I wanted to know. Thanks, Bud, for coming to see me."

I informed my staff of what I had done, what the consequences were, and that we now could begin to plan the move, without any further discussion of its merits or demerits, and I hoped without any distressing or delaying "arrières pensées." And I must say they threw themselves whole-heartedly into the very complex business of planing the building, of arranging our production program so that despite the move we could spend the money in our current budget and finish our schedule for the year, and went on to consider ways and means by which several hundred employees and their families could be uprooted from their homes and schools and be transplanted to Montreal with the minimum of apprehension and grief.

As I look back from over twenty years, I must boast that the entire operation – planning and building the new establishment, and moving the bodies – was carried out with great skill, certainly with minimum loss of personnel, and within the allowed budget. I haven't looked up the figures, but the estimate which was accepted for the new building was roughly of the magnitude of $5,300,000; we brought it into use for $5,500,000, give or take a few thousand. To exceed the original estimate by only 3 to 4 per cent in the construction of a large building, much of which by the very nature of its function had to be technical and highly specialized, seemed to me a good performance. Bob Winters, as Minister of Public Works, of course had a hand in this. He was agreeable, but firm. If we wanted to add something to the building plan that we hadn't at first thought of, Bod didn't argue with us. He took the sensible position that it was not for him to decide what was or was not needed in a building designed for the purpose of producing and distributing motion pictures. He merely told us to go ahead, but to pay for any addition we wanted by the deletion of something else we thought we could get along without.

As I recall the circumstances, the argument for the move to Montreal ran something like this. The Film Board clearly needed new and better quarters: the building on John Street, just opposite the French embassy, was an old, converted sawmill. It lacked any suggestion of modernity in the arrangement of its technical spaces and offices, and there could be no doubt that brilliant though the achievements of the Board had been under John Grierson and his successors, everyone worked there under unpleasant conditions and often crippling handicaps. It was too small: it lacked certain equipment and the room for such equipment, which a great, modern, documentary film-producing agency should have.

Granted that a new building was required, the question arose, where should it be located? To tear down the old building and use the same site for a new one would obviously put the Board out of action, or nearly so, for at least a couple of years. Should it be somewhere else in Ottawa, or was not now the time to remove the film-makers, the distributors, and the support staff to a larger centre? Irwin was convinced that a move to Montreal would have many advantages. Montreal, a large international metropolis, would afford a multiplicity of new associations, and a variety and richness of experience that could only be a stimulus to our artists. Ancillary technical facilities would be available in much greater measure than in Ottawa. Cooperation with other film companies would be possible and desirable. The Board would be centred in a much larger and more active film-making *milieu*. The French production units would be encouraged and enlivened tremendously, greatly to the advantage of this very important element of the National Film Board's responsibility, and to the increase of its impact on our French-Canadian citizens. The business of distribution, in Canada and abroad, could be carried on more efficiently from this larger centre, which, it was thought, would be much richer than Ottawa in the immediacy and variety of the means of communication.

No doubt there were other arguments, but these, I think, were the main ones. It may be that Irwin thought location in Montreal would remove the Board from the immediate pressures of the Capital's politicians; but if he did think that, I doubt if he stressed the point unduly when discussing the move with government, for, indeed, not much could have been made of it. At the time I had no idea if there existed the beginnings of a general federal government policy of decentralization, or if behind the move there was an immediate, practical political conviction that it would be smart to provide more buildings, more institutions, and more government jobs in Quebec. These were considerations that I, as a newcomer to Ottawa and as an almost apolitical man, knew and – frankly – cared little about.

Mulholland and his associates did not think these arguments convincing. Much as they all wanted a new and modern building, they pointed out that good films are not made by good buildings, but by good men. While no one wanted to continue in the seedy John Street quarters, they reminded the Government that it was here, in Ottawa, that the Film Board's great reputation had been made. John Grierson said to me, in London, before the new building had been completed,"Try to persuade your people, Trueman, that their real studios will not be in that building in Montreal, but here and there all across Canada – the sea coasts, the towns, the cities, the prairies, the lakes, the rivers, the forests, the mountains." Given some such conception as that, the Board could operate out of Ottawa as well as it could out of Montreal, or Toronto. It was not accepted by the protesters that there might be any striking advantage in the ancillary technical facilities available in Montreal, nor in association with Montreal film companies. They were simply not impressed by these arguments. That creative activity would be stimulated and enriched by metropolitan life more than by the quieter life of Ottawa and its beautiful environs they refused to believe. They could not be persuaded that political pressure had been dangerous, or that by removing to Montreal they would escape whatever there was of it, if anything. Most tellingly, perhaps, they pointed out that about half the production budget was supplied directly to the Board by government departments which wanted films made for special needs and purposes. Communication between film producer and departmental officer was quick in Ottawa, by telephone, or by meeting in consultation on the spot, easily arranged without loss of time and undue waste of energy; in short, a much more efficient association was possible in the Capital with the government departments which supplied such a high proportion of the Board's budget. The move to Montreal would mean, at least initially – and the event proved it – that a regular daily shuttle service, by car, would have to be set up between the two cities; an unprofitable expenditure of time, energy, and money.

To look after the Board's interests in general and to stimulate and arrange for the distribution of our films, we maintained offices abroad. The principal ones were located in New York, Chicago, London, and Paris. For a time, we maintained one in New Delhi. It was obviously necessary to visit these branches and familiarize myself with their personnel, the nature of their work, and their problems. Quite early on I went to London, where the office had been taken over by Karl Lochnan; the former incumbent, Jim Beveridge, had just left on a long leave of absence to make some films for Shell in, I believe, India. I remember thinking at the time that Jim Beveridge, a very able man, who had already spent some years in London, was perhaps less than wise to take on this arrangement, for it would extend rather dangerously his absence from Ottawa, where a new Commissioner, who didn't know him, had taken over, and key positions in production and distribution were being filled, of necessity, by new and younger men. ("Now there arose up a new King over Egypt, which knew not Joseph!")

My people in Ottawa advised me to hold a cocktail party in my London hotel, the Hyde Park, for the Film Board staff and for prominent film personnel, private and governmental, and representatives of business and agencies with whom we had dealings. And, of course, we invited Norman Robertson, our brilliant Canadian High Commissioner in England. I was soon made aware that something was wrong. At last, one of the English film producers said to me, quite bluntly, "There are some of us who are reluctant to go to your party." I said, "In Heaven's name why?" He answered, "Because John Grierson hasn't been invited, and he's right here in town."

I was appalled. Grierson, the founder of the Board and its first

119

Chairman, was still a name to conjure with, and clearly should have been number one on our list. I got in touch with Lochnan at once: he himself, having arrived in London only a few days before I had, had left the invitation list entirely in the hands of Beveridge, who by now had left town. "Even so," I said, "how could Grierson's name possibly have been left off?" As far as I was concerned, I had had to leave the matter to my subordinates. I wouldn't have known how to go about arranging a list for a party in London, and furthermore, I had no idea that John Grierson was in the city. I never did find out the reason for this shocking blunder.

As soon as I could, I reached Grierson on the telephone, made as much of an explanation as was possible and asked him "for God's sake" if he'd come around to my hotel and lunch with me the next day. He accepted my invitation. When I opened the door to him, he greeted me most warmly, wrung my hand, and said at once how delighted he was that I had taken over the Chairmanship of NFB. A man can't behave more handsomely than that. I ate some more crow. He waived the crow, so to speak, and walked briskly to the sideboard, inspected the bottles, and poured himself a lusty drink, after which we had an excellent lunch and some very good and, for me, illuminating conversation. It was then that John urged me to persuade my film producers not to be seduced by their new and spacious quarters in Montreal, but to think of all Canada, from sea to sea, as their studio.

I was in complete agreement with this view of Canadian documentary film-making, but I found that Mulholland and many others were burdened with what seemed to me an excess of social conscience, a do-the-people-good whether-they-like-it-or-not complex, which led them – from my point of view – into rather too much attention to "educational" films on the drug habit, crime in general, housing, and so on and on. To my mind, one film we made showing a Canadian cowboy roping a young, partially broken horse in the corral, cutting him out from his bucking, plunging fellows, bridling him, saddling him, and dashing off for a glorious hell-for-leather gallop across the prairie was worth any two of the so-called "educational" efforts we made.

This is not to say that I thought we should make no films dealing with social problems. We could scarcely avoid that. Furthermore, the Board produced brilliant documentaries of this type. As I have suggested, I felt that the balance was not being maintained. As

Grierson put it, we had a magnificent, sprawling studio nearly four thousand miles long, containing an amazing variety of scenic beauty, and of people going about the business of living, in an amazing variety of ways. I thought we should have exploited, rather more than we did, the possibilities that were there, stretched out before us.

I admit that I had no closely reasoned philosophy of documentary film-making. I suppose that by 1955, at fifty-three years of age, with a city school superintendency and two university presidencies behind me, I'd lost some of my more superficial "do-good" propensities. It seemed to me that probably the main thing – not the only thing but the main thing – we could do with the Film Board was to show the people of Canada, as only moving pictures could show, the wonder, the beauty, the variety, the excitement of their country. To see, to hear, to feel, to make significant response, and not be bothered by too much moralizing, too many lessons, too much persuasion – all this, I felt, was primarily what we ought to be helping Canadians do. That is to say, I was in favour of more art and less social propaganda.

I remember suggesting to the production boys that I'd like to see four films, not long ones, showing, with every technical skill and all the artistry at our command – and that was considerable – the Canadian Forest in Winter, Spring, Summer and Fall, using the whole extent of Canada for studio. The observation was received, as I remember it, in a kindly if somewhat embarrassed manner. Nothing came of it. I can't say where and how the line can be drawn between what I have been advocating, on the one hand, and the do-them-good, expose-the-rottenness kind of documentary, on the other. Film-makers obviously can't be blind to what's going on in our society. As I've said, I had no closely reasoned philosophy of the business. I'm perfectly aware that the professionals will gleefully pick apart my line of thought, or, perhaps, more honestly, my line of feeling. In the distressing jargon of the day, I suppose I have been giving a "gut-reaction," and not much more.

CHAPTER FIFTEEN

The work of National Film Board Chairman and Government Film Commissioner was full of interest and excitement. I was extremely proud of the Board and its accomplishments. When I first began to go abroad on Board business, I was surprised, I admit, by the welcome I got from everyone I met in the film world. In London, I once expressed to an English film-maker something of my astonishment at the cordiality of my reception. He said, "Well, surely you realize that you are sitting on top of the biggest and best documentary film-producing agency in the world." Whether or not he was wholly correct in this statement, there was no doubt whatever that the Board's reputation was very high indeed, and that much was expected of us. When I got back from two or three of these excursions, I reported this remark, and others like it, to the Minister. He made a curious response, curious, that is, to me. He said, "Trueman, don't use terms like that about the Film Board. I mean 'biggest and best documentary film-producing agency.' If that sort of thing gets around, I might very well have a question put to me in the House: 'Why should Canada have a Film Board, or indeed any other institution, that can be properly described as the 'biggest and best'?"

He was quite serious. I gathered that he himself was prepared to support the Board as it then was. Since the move to Montreal had been settled on, and the big new building was in the planning stage, it was wise, from his point of view, to jog along quietly, without provoking any potentially embarrassing questions about our rating on the international scene. I believe the current term for this posture is "keeping a low profile." I agreed to guard my tongue, but went away hoping, for the sake of Canada, that the Minister's fears were groundless. Still, he certainly knew the House and politicians, as a class, better than I did. "But why," I said to myself, "*shouldn't* a country of this size, and this wealth, and this vigour, and this promise, have something, some agency, some institution, some activity that's the best and biggest in the world?" Why not, indeed?

Harris, to tell the truth, had no serious interest in the National Film Board. He told me that he knew nothing about films; and I gathered, from the tone of the remark, that he had no intention of learning. He was quite prepared to give us the support we needed, but I could never believe that he thought our work of any great importance. He summed up the position nicely when he said to me: "What I want from you is whatever general information I should have about the Board's activities. You run the show, and keep me out of trouble in the House." Fair enough! I had only one difficult moment with him, and that came after another cabinet shuffle, which took him off to the Treasury Board, and gave me Jack Pickersgill as my Minister.

I had to present the Board's annual budget to a meeting of the appropriate Treasury body, Harris presiding. I had shown our final draft of the budget to Pickersgill, who thought it was all right, but suggested I offer it to a certain senior Treasury Board official for a final scrutiny before I ventured to put it on trial before the meeting. The official was receptive and courteous. He proposed, I recollect, that we cut about $60,000 out of a total budget of – what? – five or six million, perhaps slightly more. Since I detected nothing to fight about in this suggestion, I took the budget back to my colleagues, and made the deduction.

I think that Harris, like Winston Churchill at the University of Bristol Convocation, may have come to the meeting from a rough session in the House, because he was in a filthy temper the morning I showed up to make my little exhibition. Several Ministers were present, including my own, Jack Pickersgill, two or three of my senior colleagues, and the Treasury Board official who had proposed the deletion of $60,000, and pronounced the budget perfectly satisfactory after I had agreed to the cut. Harris took a quick look at the total, scowled, and muttered something that I couldn't quite hear. He looked at me then, and said in a most unpleasant tone, "What are you trying to do, Trueman? Supply a car to every member of the Film Board staff?" (By this time we had moved to Montreal, and new equipment charges were necessarily high.) Flabbergasted, I pulled myself together sufficiently to say, "Oh no, Sir. No, indeed!" He snapped back at me, "Well, it looks like it." I protested again, but it was obvious that he was not going to be mollified, placated, appeased, or whatever. Finally he said, "I want $250,000. taken out of this budget." Since he had raised no question about any particular expenditures – the reference to buying cars was in no way supported by anything in the document – I asked if he would leave it to me to select the items for deletion or reduction. He nodded. I picked up my papers, jerked my head at my colleagues, and swiftly left the field of this short and inglorious battle.

"What's a quarter of a million dollars?", to paraphrase the famous observation attributed, under far different circumstances – wrongly I believe – to C.D. Howe. As I have said, that was the only unpleasant moment I ever had with Walter Harris, and I couldn't hold it against him. A President of the Federal Treasury Board must surely be allowed his moments of frustration, impatience, and un-reason. I was sorry to see him leave politics.

While he was still the Film Board's Minister, Harris stood by me in a little political comedy in which I became involved, and which embarrassed me for a day or so. We were making a film in St. John's, Newfoundland. My production people told me that they wanted a narrator with professional experience and a touch of Newfoundland in his speech. They recommended, I think by long-distance telephone, a man who met these qualifications, and I told them to take him on. A day or so later, the Minister telephoned to inform me that the man we'd hired in St. John's was the Tory candidate whom Jack Pickersgill had run against and defeated in the last election: objections were being raised at both ends of the line, in St. John's and in Ottawa. I felt that I had to stand up very straight before Harris, and I said: "Mr. Minister, when we look for a man to do a job of acting or reading in a film, we don't inquire into his politics. We try to find out if he has the experience and talent and skill that we need, and if he meets our requirements we hire him. And that's the way I think it should be." To these bold words, Walter said, not altogether to my surprise, "And quite right too, Mr. Trueman," and ended the conversation.

I have sometimes wondered if the adoption of this pure and beautiful attitude was one of the political errors which Walter, some years later, recollected that he'd committed in his Ottawa days. Jack Pickersgill, of course, as everyone knows, and as he would be the first to admit, didn't play the political game by the Harris and Trueman rules. At a cocktail party somewhere, a little later, Jack asked me what the Board was up to in St. John's, and referred directly to the hiring of his defeated Tory opponent. I made some perhaps uneasy but laughing reply, refusing to be serious about the matter, but Jack was serious. He listened to my casual dismissal of the incident, and said, "That's all right, Bud. *But don't do it again!*" I broke away because I didn't think a cocktail party the right *milieu* in which to challenge a Minister of the Crown on his hiring policies. Several of my Film Board colleagues had been within hearing distance, and immediately closed in on me: "What did Pickersgill tell you not to do again?" Again I resorted to my laughing technique, dismissed the matter as nothing, and moved off for a drink.

I recall that a long time after this small encounter, I told my very good friend, Blair Fraser, about it. Blair looked at me with pity. He expressed surprise that I, a Maritimer, could be so naïve, and so ignorant of the realities underlying our political amusements. As the game was played, and had to be played, he said, any available jobs – and they weren't too plentiful – simply had to go to those who were of the true faith, and had supported successful or, for that matter, unsuccessful, candidates. That was in the bargain, that was the ancient understanding. Violation of that understanding would be disloyalty and treachery. I was suggesting a level of logic, of kindness and tolerance, even of universal good will and generosity that the political animal couldn't possibly reach. In short, Jack Pickersgill knew precisely what he was doing and why: I, said Blair, would do well to recognize the facts of life and govern myself accordingly. It was a good lesson, which I accepted, reluctantly, on the Machiavellian principle that successful government must be based on the frank recognition of what is real, in things and in men, not on blind faith in what ought to be.

But I owed a great deal to Jack Pickersgill. He was, I thought, an excellent Minister for the NFB: he was always approachable, agreeable, and helpful. After the Board's move to Montreal had been safely accomplished, I found myself swamped by the increased volume of work. It was the government's wish that I maintain my headquarters office in Ottawa. The Still-Photograph Division was located in the same building, and I began to know and understand the value of its work, and the charm and brilliance of Lorraine Monk, who has edited and directed the publication of some superb books, among the most famous being *Canada – a Year of the Land,* and *Between Friends – Entre Amis.*

I spent two or three days in Ottawa, and the rest of each working week in Montreal, and I soon got heartily sick of travelling back and forth between the two cities. My wife got sick of it too. I heard muttered sarcasms: Had I become a commercial traveller? Was I really so important that the great city of Montreal couldn't get along without my weekly attentions? And Sally found these frequent changes of her father's residence perplexing and not at all agreeable. Peter was too busy being unhappy at Carleton University to pay much attention to my flittings. But Jean has always shown a remarkable capacity for the toleration of what has to be tolerated, and an unqualified willingness to move wherever a new position beckoned me.

It became obvious to me, to my senior colleagues, and to the Minister that I needed an Assistant Commissioner to hold the fort in Montreal while I was in Ottawa, and to provide necessary and continuing liaison between me and the various departmental and divisional heads. As soon as I began to outline the new position and look for a likely candidate, I realized that certain endemic difficulties were bound to arise. Clearly, the new man would have to be a French Canadian, especially since the heads of my main departments – Production, Distribution, Finance – were all English Canadians, and I was English myself. Clearly, I would have to find him, it appeared to me, within the ranks of the Board itself. To bring in from outside somebody employed by one of the comparatively small, private-sector, Montreal film-making companies would have been like throwing a Christian to the lions. And clearly, I was going to have to promote to second-top-place in the Board someone whose present rank was lower than that of each of my senior colleagues.

As soon as word got around Ottawa that a new high-ranking position was going to be available at the Board, "interested parties" began to make suggestions. Jack Pickersgill called me to let me know that one of the French-Canadian Ministers was pushing a musician from Montreal. Would I see the fellow, and size him up? I saw him – a pleasant, genial, cigar-smoking type, who within ten minutes betrayed an abysmal ignorance of almost everything in the world but choir-conducting. I went to see Jack, not knowing how much heat and pressure were being applied to him by his colleague. I told him my story and stated my unalterable opposition to the appointment of this particular man, or of anyone remotely like him. As soon as Jack understood the facts of the case, he said "All right. Keep on looking. You can be sure I'm not going to shove anyone down your throat." You couldn't say handsomer than that!

I found my man, an excellent young man, a brilliant and genial French-Canadian, in our own ranks, Pierre Juneau, who later became the head of the CRTC, and then, after an unhappy run at politics, the head of the National Capital Commission. I could see that all this wasn't making Don Mulholland, Director of Production, very happy. But we had a frank talk or two, and Don, a highly sensitive and intelligent, though occasionally blasphemous man, came to understand and appreciate not only my point of view, but the unalterable nature of the circumstances – what I have called the endemic difficulties in Canada.

In the United States my reception was always cordial. On my visits to our New York and Chicago offices I was introduced to many people in the film-making and film-distributing world. And I made speeches, it seems to me now, without number. Again and again I was questioned about the constitution of the Board and its financing. My questioners understood quite readily our relations with the Federal Government Departments that retained us to make the special films they needed. (The Departments were supposed to use us exclusively for this purpose, but in practice they sometimes hired private companies, which, of course, were always on the look-out for Government commissions, and thought they were not given enough of them.) These relations, as I have said, were understandable: a government department wants a film which will show what has been done, let's say, to support some agricultural development in the West; the Department officers and Film Board officers meet to discuss content, length, treatment, costs, etc.; agreement is reached, and the Board in effect produces the film that the Department wants – subject, of course, to continuing professional suggestions and advice from the Board experts – and the Department pays for it. No difficulty here for our American inquirers. This sort of thing accounted for about half of our production budget.

The other half of the budget was entirely under the Board's control. We made the films we wanted to make, the films we thought ought to be made; we cut up our budgetary pie in as many pieces as we saw fit; we arranged for the distribution of the finished product –

all this without the necessity of government advice or sanction. "How," asked the Americans, "do you get away with this? Do you mean to say that the politicians don't bedevil you about the use of that uncommitted half of your budget? That you are not constantly under pressure to do this or do that for someone's political advantage?" I explained these matters as best I could, and experienced a growing pride in the Board, in the Government, and in Canada where such things were possible.

As a matter of fact – and I have said this in public more than once – I believe that Canadian government and Canadian politics have never appeared to better advantage, both abroad and at home, than in the creation and maintenance of The Canadian Broadcasting Corporation, The National Film Board, and The Canada Council. It's a staggering fact that it has been possible in Canada for Government to place huge sums of public money in the hands of these three bodies, and then leave them alone to determine, within the terms of the relevant Act, the ways in which the money should be spent. And that determination is made by governing bodies consisting almost completely of private citizens; indeed, The Canada Council board has *no* civil servant and no member of government on it whatever.

The new building on the Côte de Liesse Road proved a tremendous success. It can easily be imagined what it meant to our film-makers to have the space they needed, and the equipment, for documentary films dealing with social problems; for science films; for nature films; and for music studios, projection theatres – the lot. It was a source of constant interest to me to take a walk through the building and have a look at all the fascinating things that were going on, to talk with the personnel and get to know as many of them as I could; to drop in on a musician, Eldon Rathburn or Robert Flemming, and chat or even run through a song or two; to call on the department where "stills" were being made for instructional use in schools.

It was impossible, of course, to know all the employees in this large organization, but it seemed worthwhile to know as many as I could. If not to see the woods for the trees is to suffer defeat as an administrator, it is equally disastrous not to see the trees for the woods.

During my term of office came the advent of television on the CBC, with the consequent and immediate need for suitable television films. We at NFB realized that we were going to have to produce such films in response, we hoped, to direct commissions by the CBC, and for other markets as well. Don Mulholland came to me for a long talk. He made the point that we didn't know enough about making films suitable for display on the little glass screens that were rapidly spreading through Canadian living-rooms. What kind of films would be most in demand? Were the limitations imposed by the nature of the medium and the size of the screen great enough to force drastic changes in the selection of subjects, in technique – camera technique and direction technique? Perhaps they would be, perhaps not. Shortly after we had this conversation, a few films of ours were picked up and shown by CBC. We had to have a good look at them in use, as well as at others from other sources. Our producers and directors and cameramen would obviously have to make a serious study of this new phenomenon.

At the time when we realized we had to start the program, the Board didn't own a television set. We at once got one or two from headquarters, but this was not enough. Our own films on CBC were being shown on Sunday afternoon, after "Lassie" – scarcely prime time – and at another hour rather late on a weekday evening. It was impractical, in fact impossible, to ask the personnel concerned to come in to the Board from here, there and everywhere, in and outside Ottawa, to study television films shown on Sunday mid-afternoons and at late evening hours during the rest of the week. The only thing to do was buy a few sets and allow our production people to take them home on loan. This we did. Our total expenditure for four or five sets, at that early time, was only approximately two thousand dollars.

The news got round that NFB employees were taking government equipment home. I soon got word, I think from the Secretary of the Treasury Board, that this practice was forbidden, and that we must desist forthwith. I went to see the Secretary to explain the circumstances. We had to improvise; we had to train our film-makers in a new development of their art, and obviously not all of this training could be carried on during office hours at the plant, I said. Give us a year or more of this so-called irregular procedure, and after that television sets would become much more common, and it would be reasonable to expect that our professionals would normally want to own them. No doubt we could then cease and desist from the practice of lending. But it was ridiculous, I claimed, to ask Film Board employees – not too well-paid, God knows – to buy, at the very outset of this new departure, expensive technical equipment which they had to have if they were going to do their jobs, and which clearly they would have to use outside their regular working hours. I conceded that wives and children would use the sets. Well, so what? Even that might bring useful revelations to the film-makers, and thus be a not wholly negligible part of the training program.

My arguments were of no avail. I was informed that those of our staff who were in possession of the sets would have to pay for them out of their own pockets. I must admit that this infuriated me. I refused to make our people pay for the sets, on the grounds that they had not been responsible for their purchase: the Film Board had bought them and owned them; they were out on loan. If it was insisted that the practice had to cease, very well then – the Board would recall them, and sell them to somebody, some surplus equipment pool or whatever. This we did. My board members, all but one of whom were private citizens, numbering businessmen among them, were completely behind me in this incident, and saw no valid reason why we shouldn't lend equipment temporarily to our staff, the circumstances being what they were. I still insist that we were wholly justified in what we did, and that the prohibition was yet another example of bureaucratic lack of imagination, and stubborn, unenlightened adherence to the book of rules.

Rules and regulations are the devil. In the Film Board the foundation people were, of course, the producers, the men who made the films, without which our administrators and distributors would have had no *raison d'être*. But your film-makers are, by definition, creative people, artists. And these are precisely the sort of people who take least kindly to rules and regulations. I was prepared, myself, to allow them a good deal of latitude as far as the day-to-day observation of our little laws was concerned. What I tried to keep my eye on was the state of the year's program. Were we getting sadly behind? Was the quality of our new films falling below the fine standards that had characterized the Board's production and made it famous in the past? Were we getting into trouble with our financial masters? Were we going to fail to spend the production budget which we had so strenuously argued for? If the answer to each of these questions was a satisfactory, reassuring "no," then we were doing our job, and small trespasses could be overlooked.

It was difficult, however, for the business office to support this attitude. Ed Coristine, who ran that division, was often distressed by the fact that various members of the production division habitually came to work well after nine in the morning. *His* people were there at their desks promptly at nine, and having done a good, well-supervised day's work, left promptly at five. Then, too, the old equipment problem bothered him. From time to time he voiced his conviction that production people were taking small items of equipment home with them, not for dishonest purposes, but to use in the at-home furtherance of their assignments. There was, in fact, a kind of looseness about production which irked the tidy and extremely efficient mind of Coristine. I found it nearly impossible to prevent disastrous clashes between the two divisions. On balance, however, I felt that no matter what resentment the production people might feel about what they regarded as carping and wholly unnecessary criticism, Ed's management of our business office was so efficient, his knowledge of our finances and his awareness of the relations we had to observe with Treasury Board were so good, that he had to be supported. He kept us out of trouble. And that, believe me, was a blessing indeed.

I talked with him from time to time, and I think I was able to make some gains. I pointed out to him the creative, artistic nature of these film-makers; however slack they might be about punctuality and the use of Board equipment, they were the people who without overtime wages or salary, remained late in the building for long, long hours, to work on films that had aroused their special excitement; in the last two or three months of the fiscal year the production offices and labs were filled at night with men and women striving, by their own choice, to complete a full and difficult program. In short, I tried to persuade him, with some success I believe, that in an organization like ours, what came out the other end was what mattered above anything else.

If our product was ample and of high quality, we should endure the petty annoyances occasioned by rule violations: we not only should, we must. There is no other way to work satisfactorily with creative, and, admittedly, sometimes eccentric, people. They were just as disciplined as anyone else. You don't get distinguished films from careless, undisciplined people. But the modes of their discipline, which is self-imposed, are their own, and they have to be recognized, tolerated, and at times, one might feel, endured. It was unthinkable that I should impose rules on Norman McLaren, for example, a film genius if ever there was one. This remarkable man, modest and self-effacing, would come into my office at budget time

and make a soft-voiced suggestion that, if it was possible and altogether convenient, he would like to have X dollars at his disposal in
the coming year. And the sum he asked for always seemed to me
remarkably small. Of course he got his money. And as far as I was
concerned, he was then entirely free to work when and where and
how he pleased. The films he made, as everyone who knows anything
about film will agree, have provided abundant justification of the
freedom he was allowed. His work was not purchasable in terms of
money, or explicable in terms of hours of labour. Would I try to
discipline Guy Glover? Perish the thought! Or Bob Flemming? Or
Eldon Rathburn? Or Tom Daly? Or Nick Balla?

I admit that at times I was forced to ask myself what the devil I was
doing there, at the Film Board; I, who was not a film-maker and, up to
that time, not even a serious film fan. I thought of John Grierson,
wrapped up almost totally in the conceiving and making of documentary films. He and Harold Innis, both on a Manitoba Royal
Commission for Adult Education, which I chaired, were at opposite
poles. Harold, to tell the truth, wasn't much concerned for adult
education; John, on the other hand, seemed concerned for almost
nothing else.

Obviously, then, my role at NFB could not be, for the most part,
anything like Grierson's. What was there I could do that would be
valuable and have some hope of success? In the first place, I could try
to keep the institution out of serious trouble with government and
with the general public. This is not as easy as it sounds. The trick was
not to avoid criticism; that was impossible and even inadvisable. No:
it was to be progressive, innovative, and useful without at the same
time compromising our independence, and without having to carry
on our program in a constant state of warfare. I think, on the whole,
that I was successful in this respect, owing greatly to the sane
intelligence of my principal colleagues, and their over-all desire to
cooperate with me. I could do my best to keep morale high. This
meant, as far as the staff was concerned, my recognition of their
merits and of the nature and aims of the Board itself; a fair "do" all
round; being accessible in my office; getting to know and understand
as many individuals as possible; not taking peace and harmony for
granted, but working as best I could to iron out difficulties and
prevent, by intelligent anticipation, events and circumstances that
could lead to bad feeling and production delays. It is not given to

anyone to score a hundred per cent in this role. Still, I recall NFB morale in those days with modest satisfaction – but no more, certainly, than modest satisfaction.

As a more nearly direct contribution to the success of the film-making program, there were certain things I could do. It could not be my function to be much of an idea man. But then, that was scarcely necessary. I was surrounded by brilliant, creative people who were bursting with ideas. I could go over the proposed program for the year with my production and distribution colleagues, and exercise, reasonably I hope, some power of selection, now and then advocate caution or restraint, and even – though rarely, I admit – utter a flat "no." But it seemed to me that my principal function, surrounded, as I was by a host of lively, thinking, dreaming, provocative minds, was to be a clearer-away of obstacles, creating and presiding over a situation in which desirable things could happen with a minimum of the frustrating delays which can be caused by difficulties not foreseen or removed.

As I look back to this experience, which lasted four years, I suspect that I stayed with the Board just about long enough. A man of my type could make, and I think I did make, a certain kind of limited contribution of the sort I have described. But that contribution, as I have said, had to be limited. The move from Ottawa to Montreal was made during my period in office. Naturally that took up a great deal of the total time I spent with the Board. I can't maintain that in any sense *I* moved the Board to Montreal. The most I can claim is that the total situation, to which I certainly contributed something, was such that the move was accomplished with rather less trouble than might have been anticipated. But the main credit for this difficult operation must go to my colleagues. I think with especial gratitude of Gerry Graham, our principal engineer, who toiled terribly over the business, and of Ray Payne, head of our laboratories. Dozens of names come to mind as I recall those busy days, the names of those who had helped to make the Board and were continuing to keep its reputation high: film makers – Colin Low, Roman Kroiter, Roger Blais, Nick Balla, Michael Spencer, Gudren and Morten Parker, Jacques Bobet, David Bairstow; musicians – Eldon Rathburn, Robert Flemming; distribution staff Dooley Gray, Charlie Marshal, Len Chatwin, Bill Cosmann; support staff Marjorie McKay of Production Research, Lucille Bishop, Vera Steacy, Eva Pearce, and my secretary, Reta Kilpatrick,

133

who gave me the kind of sympathetic understanding and help to which Gladys Yelland and Bing McKay had made me accustomed. The National Film Board, is, and has always been, an exciting institution, with exciting, difficult, creative people. I look back to the four years of my Chairmanship as an adventure, and an education, which would have diminished me indeed, had I missed it.

CHAPTER SIXTEEN

One Saturday in April, in 1957, I was in Toronto attending a meeting. When I went back to my hotel room at about 4:30 in the afternoon, a message was waiting: would I call Operator so-and-so in Ottawa. I made the call and was immediately connected with my "party." And my party was Mr. Louis St. Laurent, the Prime Minister.

"Is that you, Doctor Trueman? This is Louis St. Laurent speaking."

"Hello, Mr. Prime Minister! What can I do for you?"

"Dr. Trueman, you will have heard of the Canada Council?"

"Oh yes, Sir. Yes indeed."

"We are about to establish the Canada Council. We should like you to be the Director. Are you interested?"

"Yes, indeed, Mr. St. Laurent. Most certainly."

"Good! Mr. Brooke Claxton will be the Chairman. When are you returning to Ottawa?"

"This evening, Sir, on the late train."

"Very well, Dr. Trueman. See Mr. Claxton as soon as you can."

"Splendid! Thank you very much, Mr. Prime Minister."

"Not at all, Dr. Trueman. Good-bye."

In 1951 the Royal Commission on National Development in the Arts, Letters and Sciences, under the chairmanship of Vincent Massey, recommended the establishment of a Canada Council for the Encouragement of the Arts, Humanities, and Social Sciences. No doubt the final impetus to create the Council, in 1957, was the windfall for the Federal Government of approximately a hundred million dollars in the form of succession duties realized from the estates of Izaak Walton Killam and Sir James Dunn, both of whom had died in 1956. On March 28, 1957, the Canada Council Act was given assent. The arts were defined as "architecture, the arts of the theatre, literature, music, painting, sculpture, the graphic arts, and other similar creative and interpretive activities." [2] The humanities and the social sciences were not given definition.

A hundred million dollars were made over to the new Council. Half of this sum was placed in an Endowment Fund, the earnings of which were designated for the support of a program of grants, scholarships, and loans. The other half was placed in a Capital Grants Fund, the principal and earnings of which were designated for capital assistance "to universities and similar institutions of higher learning in respect of building construction projects." [9]

This was the new-born institution of which the Prime Minister had asked me to be the Director.

The telephone conversation was just as brief as I have reported it, although I may have got a word wrong here and there. It may seem odd that I so quickly accepted the Prime Minister's offer. But I had been fascinated by the Massey Commission report, and had watched the press eagerly for indications that the Government was planning to act on its recommendation that a Council be established in support of the Arts, Humanities, and Social Sciences. Whether it was conceited of me, or mere day-dreaming, it seemed to me that I had certain qualifications for a senior post in the organization: administrative experience, academic training and extended association with universities and their scholars; special interest in literature, considerable training in music, a general interest in the arts, and certainly some experience in making grants and awarding scholarships to students in many disciplines.

When Bob Winters had telephoned to offer the Chairmanship of NFB, I confess that one of the attractions of moving to Ottawa was precisely that the new Canada Council might one day be established. As I told Winters, I was deeply interested in the Film Board, but I scarcely expected to spend a long, long period in its service. I felt then and I continued to feel that I could make a useful contribution to the Board, but not over a long, sustained period. To pitch in and do my best for NFB was my purpose. If, after a fair and reasonable interval, something else came up, as Bob Winters suspected it might; something in which I had a special interest, then I would consider it and determine where I could make the better contribution. And so I had gone to Ottawa, excited about my new job at the Film Board and its opportunities, but by no means committed to it for years and years to come.

On Sunday morning I called Brooke Claxton, whom I knew, and who was a neighbour of mine in Rockcliffe. We had a cordial and satisfactory meeting. I recall saying that this was happening very suddenly; I had been going all-out for some time, and I'd like a few days between jobs, to catch my breath.

"Certainly you must have a breather," he said. Early the next morning he called me at home before I had left for downtown, to tell me that he had his eye on office space that might possibly be suitable for the new Council. Would I come along and inspect it? Of course I agreed. I got away from Brooke before noon, and took up my Film Board affairs again, for the rest of the day.

That evening, April 15, 1957, the Order-in-Council was signed, appointing the Chairman, the Vice-Chairman, the other members of Council, the Director and the Associate Director. Consequently on Tuesday morning I was no longer the Chairman of the National Film Board and Government Film Commissioner. Quick work! It left me in an embarrassing situation. I had abruptly ceased to have authority to do anything at all for the Board; issue instructions, sign a contract, take on staff. And, of course, Mr. Claxton had no notion of giving me a breather. We kept on looking for office space, and finally got what we wanted in the Victoria Building at 140 Wellington Street, just opposite the Parliament Buildings. I cleared my desk at NFB, put some papers together, labelled them "For the new Chairman," and took off.

The office space which we had engaged was not available until June. As we started our work, there were only four of us on the staff: I as Director; the Associate Director, Eugène Bussière; the Acting Secretary of the Council and, in the early days, my personal secretary, Lillian Breen; and Gaby Boudreault, Eugène's secretary. Where were we to meet to start the wheels rolling? I was surprised, to put it mildly, when Brooke Claxton told me that Mr. St. Laurent had suggested we make use of the Prime Minister's offices in the Centre Block of the Parliament Buildings, since he would not be occupying them for two or three months to come. In we moved. I took over Mr. St. Laurent's office and sat at his desk, regarding with some astonishment the grandeur of my surroundings.

I realized that the development of a Council program to deal with the activities of artists and scholars would present many difficulties, and require ingenious innovation, diplomacy, tact, and a delicate tread – at least now and then – and courage. I recalled that in 1956 I once expressed to Bob Bryce, Clerk of the Privy Council, my great interest in the proposed Canada Council. "Good God, Bud," he exclaimed, "you wouldn't want to get mixed up in a crazy thing like that, would you?" But I had no hesitation whatever. How could I reject an opportunity to take a hand in fashioning a program of such exciting interest, and of such profound importance to Canada?

The first meeting of the Council, which consisted of the Chairman, Mr. Claxton, the Vice-Chairman, Père Georges Henri Lévesque (wonderful man) and nineteen other appointed members, took place in a large room in the Parliament Building, in the Centre Block. We had invited to our inaugural session, among others, representatives of the Carnegie Corporation, the Rockefeller Foundation, the Ford Foundation, External Affairs, the Canadian Social Sciences Research Council, the Humanities Research Council of Canada, and the Canada Foundation. The Americans congratulated us, and pointed out that in our first year, our income being what it would be, we could make grants exceeding the total amount of all the grants which the three American foundations had made in Canada over a long period. They were cautious about giving us the advice which, of course, we wanted. But I remember with amusement that Alan Pifer, now President of the Carnegie Corporation, suggested that when we had to refuse a request for money, we should not explain, but simply state that the Council would not make the grant. As a tactful intimation of the Council's refusal, he said that the following formula made the point: "Dear Sir: We have nothing but praise for your application!"

It took only a little experience of being "philanthropoids" – Brooke loved this jocular name for his function – to convince us that it was indeed wise not to explain. But it was a counsel of perfection after all. *Some* explanations we had to give, where they concerned over-all policy, and sheer financial incapacity to meet extravagant and even outrageous demands. But in the case of refusal based on our judgment that the applicant, an individual or an institution, was second-rate or even third-rate in performance, was unpromising; was, in the case of an institution, badly run by inadequate personnel – no. Such explanations could only stimulate resentment, argument, and long and futile correspondence.

We stuck very closely to this principle, but I recall one occasion in which our hand was forced. We had been making a fairly generous annual grant to an institution in Toronto – I shan't name it – which in our judgment was bound on a dangerous course. Their most recent application we had refused, as courteously as possible, but firmly. The Toronto papers picked up the story and accused the Council of unfairness, of showing partiality for others, of bias against Toronto, of arrogance, and I don't know what else. I was telephoned by a reporter, I think from the *Toronto Star*, and given what I'm sure he thought was some pretty straight talk. I kept my temper, however, and said that while we regretted the necessity of our decision, we were sure we were right; in fact, were not unduly perturbed by the hullabaloo that was being raised in the press. This last remark was printed, and further accusations of Ottawa bureaucracy, conceit, and pig-headedness were aimed at us, and at me. So much was being made of the situation and it became so unpleasant that I went to Brooke Claxton to suggest that we could do the Council some good and perhaps even provide some useful education to other institutions by breaking our rule and making a public explanation of our refusal. He agreed, and I put together a careful letter, which Brooke edited, and sent it off to the Toronto papers. The facts were that the institution in question was in a financial mess, which had steadily grown more and more serious over the past two or three years. Any amount that we could give them would not be sufficient to bail them out, or keep the bank off their back even for a few months. Their books made it perfectly evident that a grant in response to their current application would be consumed in debt payment, go down the drain with the rest of their income, and leave the situation basically unchanged. Clearly it would be an irresponsible use of public money to provide them with further sums. The decision to explain proved a right one. The next day the newspapers abruptly changed their tune. "No wonder," they said, "the Canada Council has refused to continue its annual grant!" We were off the hook, but at the price of putting the institution there in our place. Nevertheless, the principle of not explaining was a good one, and we adhered to it in the vast majority of instances, even when we were seriously challenged.

It was an unhappy fact that in most of my administrative jobs I had felt too far removed from genuine and intimate participation in the programs that the institutions were designed to carry on – from scholarship, from research, from teaching, from film-making. I had little direct association with what came out the other end. In the

Canada Council all was different. From the start I was closely involved, not only in over-all administration, but in the judgment of applications, and the making of basic, day-to-day program decisions of one kind or another. Indeed, the Council adopted as one of its by-laws that all requests for grants must be presented to it by the Director, who received them from individuals and organizations here and there across Canada, and examined them with the help of his colleagues and special committees. That is to say, no member of the Council, not even the Chairman and the Vice-Chairman, was permitted to originate an application on behalf of any individual or organization, and move its acceptance. When it is considered that there were only twenty-one members to represent all of Canada, the wisdom of this by-law is evident. It took a little time for the members to understand clearly what their proper functions were, and the ways in which those functions were necessarily limited. For instance, there were a few members who, not unnaturally, at first regarded themselves as the special representatives of the particular communities from which they came, and as charged with responsibility for getting as much from the Council for those communities as they reasonably could.

The analogy with members of the House of Commons and their constituencies was obviously false; such an approach could not be made to work. If a Council member came, for instance, from Winnipeg and regarded himself as chiefly responsible for working in the interests of that city, then why was there not a representative from Saskatoon, and Nelson, and Sarnia, and Trois Rivières, and Sydney, and Saint John, and Three Tree Creek, and wherever? But we soon got this kind of thing sorted out. The French-Canadian members were naturally bound to keep a sharp eye on the English-French ratio of money paid out, and of numbers of scholarships, and grants to organizations. So were the English Canadians. But as the Council grew more familiar with its rôle and with the nation-wide problems it had to face, a most satisfactory national, non-regional attitude developed.

One difficulty that faced the French-Canadian members arose precisely from the M.P.-Constituency analogy held so strongly by the French-Canadian applicants. More commonly than anywhere else in Canada, the Québécois regarded the Council member as his representative in the "House," and believed that he was there to secure advantage for his constituents. The difficulty revealed itself almost amusingly – at least so it appears to me now, as I look back some twenty or more years – as a direct consequence of our no-explanation policy. The French-Canadian member knew only too well that when he got back to Montreal or Quebec, disappointed applicants would soon be on the telephone asking why they had not been given their grants. "What am I to say to him? What shall I tell her? I must have some explanation of why the applications have been refused." Brooke Claxton replied, not much to their content at first, "You say that the Council has limited funds in your category, far more than the Council could possibly support, and that the selection committee did not include your name in the list of the relatively few it was able to recommend for assistance. That's all you can say. That's all any of us can say." Perhaps this seems a little harsh, unnecessarily obdurate. But consider the alternatives. As soon as the Council begins to make explanations, no matter how well dressed up in the courtesy of circumlocution, inevitably something will be said which, stripped of disguise, means: "You are not considered as intelligent as X, Y, and Z," "The committee was not much impressed by your talents," or "You were not considered by the committee to sing, dance, paint, act, or write, as well as those who were given awards," or "The Committee did not consider you sufficiently promising to justify a grant," or "Your academic record is disappointing," or "The committee did not find what your referees say about you very convincing." All such explanations would be bound to raise sharp questions and provoke resentment and vigorous denial and correspondence. Far better to use the Claxton formula, taking shelter, so to speak, under the financial limitations of the program and the large number of applicants, many of whom, no doubt estimable people, would always have to be turned down because of lack of funds.

But, as I said, some decisions had to be explained, explained in the general policy statements made in our publications, and in speeches and interviews which we gave in every province of Canada, and in correspondence with individuals who represented petitioning organizations. We had to make it clear that although the Council had been set up with magnificent assets of one hundred million, half of that was to be paid out to universities for buildings, and the other half was to constitute a continuing endowment fund, the interest on which was to be used for grants to organizations and for scholarships to individuals occupied in one way or another, in the arts, humanities, and social sciences. That income, in my time at the Council, never rose above – say – three and a half million dollars. Taking three million as a round sum to work with, we had approximately a million dollars each for the arts, the humanities, and the social sciences. These sums distributed over Canada, though useful, were manifestly inadequate.

As I recall those early days, the greatest difficulty was created by applications from the arts groups. There was a body of opinion outside the Council, and within the Council too, at first, that what we ought to do – indeed, *had* to do – was support "grass-roots" endeavours. We should forget about the big organizations in the big cities – symphony orchestras, theatres, ballet companies, art galleries, and the like – where it was presumed that wealth was at hand and most easily accessible. We should give our encouragement to beginnings, however humble, in the smaller towns and cities, and thus help to create the rich soil in which new and little plants could take root and flourish. In this way the Council would stimulate and support a national disposition to value and cultivate the arts: music, dance, ballet, theatre. The theory sounds good – fundamental, genuinely philanthropic, and humane. In practice, however, it was impossible.

One of the first things I had to learn was that a decision to recommend a grant to the Council must depend not only on the virtues of the organization that applied, but on the size and nature of the category the application represented. In all logic and fairness, what we were prepared to do for one member of a category we must be prepared to do for others, provided they were of at least roughly equal merit. For example, before making a grant to a small choir in a small town we had to ask ourselves: "to how many other small choirs in how many other small towns are we committing our support?" And if we supported small choirs in small towns, would we not be committed to support small orchestras, string quartets, small brass bands, small theatres, small art galleries in hundreds and hundreds of small towns in eastern, western, and central Canada? A grass-roots program of this type was clearly impractical: we didn't have, and were unlikely ever to have, enough money to finance it. Any such attempt would have meant splitting up our meagre funds into countless little sums: a hundred dollars here, two hundred there, and three hundred somewhere else. Such a procedure would have been almost completely useless in that it wouldn't have enabled anything to grow and improve, and a large proportion of the money would have gone to the support of hopeless mediocrity. And as Sam Steinberg, who proved an excellent member of the Council, was over-heard to say to his neighbour at an early meeting, "I don't think we are here to support mediocrity."

The same line of reasoning applied with equal force to our program of academic awards to individuals. We had to confine ourselves to post-graduate students: pre-doctoral candidates, and post-doctoral scholars. It would have been impossible to make any useful contribution by dividing a few hundred thousand dollars into innumerable tiny awards for the undergraduate category. The numbers involved would have defeated us.

I'm trying to make clear the nature of some of the problems that confronted the Council from the moment it sat down to deliberate on the difficult business of giving money away, imaginatively, fairly, and helpfully. For me, certainly, these early confrontations were fascinating. It was refreshing to be so deeply involved in working out the solutions; to feel that my knowledge and experience were not being applied solely to comparatively remote acts of administration, but were being used directly, in the actual production of what the Council was created to produce: in general terms, a broad program of grants and scholarships calculated to encourage the study and the production of works in the Arts, Humanities, and Social Sciences in Canada, and in particular terms, actual selection of organizations and individuals to receive the awards.

I recall with some amusement an Hungarian refugee whose lordly application we had refused. In a curt letter, he stated bluntly that he had no time and no use for our red tape: he would fill out no forms; we should appeal to any of the provincial superintendents of education – he did not care which – for information about him and his work, the implication being that we would learn various things redounding greatly to his credit. We took him at his word and wrote to three superintendents. The first reply we got stated that the young man was unknown in that office. The second said that his name was on record but the office had nothing like enough information about him to justify comment. The third informed us that indeed his name was known, but that under no circumstances would the superintendent recommend him for a Council grant. Accordingly, we turned him down.

A month or so later the young man appeared on Nathan Cohen's CBC panel, Fighting Words. (Nathan had been a student of mine at Mount Allison, back in the thirties.) Nathan opened the show, as was his custom, by directing a question, without preliminary, to one of his guests. On this occasion he said to the young man – I'm sure with mischievous intent – "Well, Mr. Blank, what do you think of the Canada Council?" "It stinks!" was the reply. Shortly after that, a young man opened my office door in Ottawa, having brushed past my secretary without speaking to her, swaggered in, sat down and told me his name. It was Mr. Blank. He thought, he informed me, he'd like to see me, in my luxurious office, with my huge salary, controlling vast sums of money, and refusing grants to gifted people who deserved and needed them.

No communication was possible. I could not betray his referees by revealing that they had refused to recommend him. After a few minutes I was able to get rid of him – without exercising violence. I have often wondered what became of him; whether he long survived in a world so unappreciative of his talents, and held in such contempt by him for its ingratitude.

Brooke Claxton as our first Chairman gave the Council excellent guidance and leadership. At that time, retired from politics, he was the head of the Metropolitan Life Insurance Company in Canada. A stimulating personality, a man of strong opinions and of imagination, devoted to the interests of the new Council, he was determined to set it firmly on the road he thought it should follow. In my opinion his judgment was almost always sound. His view was national in its scope. He clearly saw the pitfalls into which we could blunder. He had no patience with softness, with making grants out of good feeling alone, out of sympathy, say, with a struggling organization which, however admirable its intentions, gave little promise either of financial stability or artistic success. While he did not at all believe in the grass-roots policy which I have referred to, he was perhaps inclined to be over-wary of giving the big organizations too much, merely because they *were* big and had the reputation and the clout to make their applications difficult to refuse.

For my part, I always felt that we should have done more than we did for Stratford in its early days. I was strongly convinced that the Shakespeare Festival was one of the most important and promising artistic ventures ever promoted in Canada, and that its reputation was improving so rapidly that it would be good for the Council's credit to be one of the Festival's principal supporters. I dare say Brooke may have been right, however, in his more cautious appraisal of our responsibilities. We certainly were of help to Stratford in those years, 1957-1965, and the Festival continued to grow in stature, even if I, as Director, was convinced that the Council should have provided larger grants than it did.

Brooke chaired the Council with great firmness. Furthermore, he was not the kind of chairman who contented himself merely with presiding over the four or five sessions we had each year. His office at the Metropolitan was only a few yards down the street from the Victoria Building. Consequently it was easy for me to keep in close touch with him, and for him to keep a close eye on me.

I admired Brooke tremendously, and I liked him, although I never could feel that I was close to him in a personal way. On several occasions I couldn't agree with his handling of individual applications, but I always approved, strongly, the over-all policies which he insisted the Council should adopt and follow. We were extremely fortunate to have him as Chairman during those early days of the Council's existence. Strength and wisdom and commonsense were greatly needed as this new departure in a national endeavour to do what had to be done for the arts, humanities, and social sciences got started. And he had these qualities in full measure. He died, too young, in 1960, after a long and painful illness. We put up a plaque in the Victoria Building. I composed the message that I thought it should convey:

"This plaque has been placed here in memory of the Honourable Brooke Claxton, Q.C., P.C., B.C.L., LL.D., D.C.M., and in recognition of the wise and resolute leadership that he gave to The Canada Council, of which he was the first Chairman, April 15, 1957 to June 13, 1960."

"A la mémoire de l'honorable Brooke Claxton, C.R., C.P., B.C.L., LL.D., D.C.M., qui a donné une direction sage et résolu au Conseil des Arts du Canada, dont il a été le premier président, 15 avril 1957-13 juin, 1960."

CHAPTER SEVENTEEN

Getting the Canada Council office organized was great fun. I was determined that we should present, from the start, a good image to the government and to the public. Many people, I found, referred to us as "The Arts Council" – indeed our official French title was "Le Conseil des Arts." Would we do mad, far-out things? Would we be inefficient and irresponsible and look like the popular stereotypes of artist and professor? Would we manage money carelessly and invest it unwisely? (After all, the Council had been given outright the considerable sum of one hundred million dollars.) I give, with considerable satisfaction, a general answer based on something C.J. Mackenzie wrote to me after he had been made a member of the Council. C.J. had some misgivings about his appointment, since his academic background had been engineering and science, and his distinguished occupation for many years had been the presidency of the National Research Council. He professed some doubts about his capacity to be of much use on a Council devoted to the encouragement of the Arts, Humanities, and Social Sciences. (I smiled inwardly about this: C.J. would have been useful on *any* council dealing with *any* matters, at *any* time.) He came to his first meeting, he told me, afraid that he might discover an "arty," fussy-professorial atmosphere, in sharp contrast with the more disciplined approaches made by the NRC to its responsibilities for the sciences. To his great pleasure, he said, he found a tight ship, efficient office practice, an over-all atmosphere of dedicated and controlled concern, and clear indications that we knew what we were about.

But to get back to the organization of the Council: credit for the state of affairs which C.J. found so satisfactory must go, first of all, to Brooke Claxton, the Chairman, and then to an excellent group of

Council members, to our superb Finance Committee, headed by Graham Towers, and to three Council officers: Doug Fullerton, the Treasurer; Lillian Breen, the Secretary; and Peter Dwyer, Head of the Arts Division. Of course, Associate Director Eugène Bussière and I were quite prepared to claim credit for the success with which we exercised our over-all responsibilities for organization and morale, and for contributions to policy-making. We were not too modest for that. But I'm sure Eugène would agree with my attribution of a great deal of basic credit to those I have named. From the start, our money was handled with great skill. Our rate of interest on investment was high, higher indeed than that for most philanthropic foundations we knew of. Our endowment fund steadily appreciated in market value and, in consequence, so – if very slowly – did our annual income.

From the start, Associate Director Eugène Bussière and I were on harmonious terms. Eugène, an excellent man, had a great interest in UNESCO, and especially in the early days of the Council pitched in and did first rate pioneering work as we sought to carry out the instructions we had received from the government. These, basically, were as follows: "...to take steps to establish a National Commission for UNESCO...," and to "provide the Secretariat for the National Commission...." Eugène was appointed Secretary, and three members of Council were designated to sit as the Commission: Dr. N.A.M. Mackenzie, Dr. J.E. Leddy, and Madame Alfred Paradis. We couldn't have had a better team. Very soon after the organization was set up, Eugène was invited by the Director General of UNESCO to visit headquarters in Paris; while in Europe on this errand he attended the regional conference of the European National Commission in Dubrovnik, Yugoslavia. After his return he worked most effectively on the program and on securing adequate documentation. Indeed, all his work at the Council, largely in relation to the social sciences, was of a high order.

We were very lucky to secure the services of Doug Fullerton and Lillian Breen. The Chairman sent Doug to see me while I was still splendidly enthroned behind Prime Minister St. Laurent's office desk in the Centre Block. We chatted generally for a few minutes, and then Doug brought up a matter he had on his mind. He said, "Of course I st-st-st-stutter." He waited for me to say something. What I said was "That makes no difference to me at all. What does make a difference is whether in this job it will worry *you*". "Oh, h-h-hell, no!" he replied, an endearing observation that, as far as I was concerned, sealed the bargain. He took over the business side of our operation, and handled it with great competence and devotion to the best interests of the Council. He was an outspoken officer, and never hesitated to tell me what he thought, not only about financial matters, but about other aspects of the program. And what he thought was always worth listening to, even though I could not always agree with him.

Lillian Breen, also sent by Claxton, came to see me, as Doug had, in the Prime Minister's office. She was a woman of considerable experience in a senior, private-secretarial capacity, and had the reputation of being second to none in ability and in the quality of her work. I was delighted to have her on the staff. She started working as my secretary, but after we had begun to hold meetings and acquire necessary staff, she was confirmed in the post of Secretary to the Council. She also acted as Office Manager. She had a clear head, a gift for organization, a strong backbone, and great charm of manner. She was not inclined to put up with nonsense from anyone, including the Director. More than once she came into my office, her Irish dander up, eyes flashing, to report on some staff delinquency, or to protest against some procrastination of mine. What a woman! A remarkably able and competent officer, loyal to the nth degree, and a true friend, she made a significant contribution to the launching of the Council and to its navigation for something more than eight years.

I suppose the most brilliant officer we had, during my time, was Peter Dwyer. I first met him on an *ad hoc* committee set up by the Government to examine the need for a big auditorium in Ottawa, where opera, ballet, and symphony orchestras could be provided with suitable conditions of performance. I for one was heartily sick of going to the old Capital moving picture theatre, so poorly lighted that you couldn't read a program, with an inadequate stage, when I wished to see ballet and opera, and listen to orchestral concerts. Clearly the city needed a good, big theatre-cum-concert hall in the worst way. I recall that the committee discussed the situation in great detail, and boldly admitted that it was talking about an expenditure of five, six, or even seven million dollars. I can only be grateful that the project expanded, as ultimately it did, and at whatever cost, to give us the National Arts Centre, which is not only magnificently equipped for opera, ballet, orchestra, and theatre, but to my mind is among the two or three best pieces of architecture in Ottawa. It has made a long-awaited and, without doubt, a much-needed and valuable contribution to popular entertainment and high art, not only for Ottawa, but for the nation at large.

When the Council began to feel the need of someone to give special and undivided attention to the Arts program – our scholarships for individual performing and creative artists, and our grants in aid of organizations – Peter Dwyer seemed easily the best person we could lay hands on. He had been working, I believe, in the offices of the Privy Council. Peter was a brilliantly intelligent fellow, sensitive, even somewhat high-strung, well trained in literature and much interested in the arts generally, and well informed about them, a keen observer and judicious critic.

Peter's discharge of his responsibilities as Head of the Arts division was eminently successful from the start. His judgment of individual applications was always shrewd and sound, and his capacity to see the Canadian arts in the largest, most comprehensive context was, in my opinion, masterly. He very soon knew what the national situation was in symphonic music, theatre, opera, ballet, and painting; what the basic problems were, and what would be the wisest use of the Council's resources in an attack on those problems. It didn't take him long to discover that our rôle as encourager of the arts was greatly limited by lack of funds, but it was always a treat to see the intelligent and highly discerning way in which he split up his million dollars-or-so among the innumerable hungry.

A man of great charm and great tact, he must have had scores of friends and admirers across Canada by the time he had travelled from coast to coast, to talk with conductors, directors, producers, curators *et al.* in all our major cities. He had another talent, a very conspicuous talent. He "wrote like an angel." During his years at the Council no annual report from any other source in Ottawa matched his for readable style, for wit and humour, for apt quotation, for persuasiveness, and for sane and incisive comment on the business at hand.

Peter and I worked closely together. All recommendations for scholarships and grants in aid of the arts were, of course, made to the Council by me. In preparation for Council meetings, Peter and I consulted in minute detail. Now and then I had to hold him back from some impractical venture, or even flatly to reject an idea. But we never had any difficulties of understanding, and our conception of what ought to be done and what could be done with the funds at our disposal came to be as nearly one as could have been expected, in the special and difficult nature of a national program for the arts.

He, like me, was a Shakespeare buff. It was my custom on April 23rd to send him a message: "Dear Peter: Many happy returns of Shakespeare's birthday!"

When, some years after I left the Council, Peter was made Director, I didn't know whether to feel glad or sorry. Naturally I was glad to see him given the recognition that he so much deserved, and I had no doubts that he would give sagacious leadership in the affairs of the Council, *in toto,* not only in the Arts. On the other hand, I knew that he was a high-strung man who found it difficult to avoid taking his job to bed with him, and that he was more distressed over personnel problems – of which there are always at least a few – than was consistent with sustained peace of mind. I felt sure that the job would be very hard on him. I can't say that the strain of his directorial duties shortened his life, although I have always suspected that it did. His death – in his fifties, I believe – was a great loss to the Council and to all the institutions with which he had such a fruitful and long, but alas! not long enough, association.

Claude Bissell, President of the University of Toronto, was the next Chairman of the Canada Council, after Brooke Claxton. He did a superb job. Claude is a fine scholar, English literature being his particular discipline; he has wide interests in the three areas of the Council's responsibilities: the arts, humanities, and social sciences. He had senior administrative experience, as President of Carleton University and then of the University of Toronto. He knew what it meant to be a Chairman: he knew how to handle a meeting – get the business done, allow a reasonable time to the board members for the expression of personal opinion, give careful consideration to points of view other than his own, maintain consistency of policy in the making of grants and scholarships, and keep the peace. He kept a sufficiently careful eye on the running of the ship, but left the officers to carry out what were obviously their responsibilities, and what they obviously could best and most quickly do. He contrived to have this relationship with the officers without provoking Council members to make the hoary and infuriating complaint I have heard so often; namely, that the board was simply acting as a rubber-stamp for decisions and actions of the employees.

I was particularly appreciative of the no-nonsense business arrangements which Claude Bissell made for regular consultation between us. Before each meeting I went to see him in his office at the University of Toronto, taking with me the agenda as I and the other officers had prepared it. We met at eleven in the morning. His secretary had been told that we were not to be interrupted for the next hour and a half, either by telephone calls or by visitors. We went over the agenda item by item; consequently, before every meeting the Chairman was familiar with each application that was to come up, knew my opinions and the other officers' opinions, and in what way these various requests related, or did not relate, to the established policies of the Council. He always took me to the York Club for lunch, where we completed our consultation on any matter which we felt needed a little more thought.

Claude endeared himself to Eugène Bussière and me when he first visited the Council's chambers in Ottawa. He drew us aside and asked if we were generally happy about our lot, and particularly, if we were content with our salaries. Here he touched upon a sore point, certainly with me. When I moved over to the Council from NFB, Brooke Claxton allowed me a salary increase from fifteen to sixteen thousand, and with this I had to be content, although I felt that I had not been treated at all generously. I found out, very soon, that Brooke hated to pay salaries. In time I got another thousand, and there I stuck: Eugène was, I think, at two thousand below me.

Claude immediately took steps to remedy the situation. After Eugène and I had discreetly withdrawn from the next Council meeting, the members voted to raise my salary by three thousand dollars, and Eugène's by two. We were both very grateful for the Board's action, not only because we needed the money, but because the motion was in a very practical way a vote of confidence in our work. The catch was that for the Director and Associate Director, the increase had to be approved by our Minister, such being the stipulation in the Act. (All the other employees were appointed by the Council, and the Council paid their salaries without reference to the Government.) Our Minister was the Prime Minister, who at that time was the Hon. John George Diefenbaker. After a delay of a couple of weeks, we received the astonishing news that Mr. Diefenbaker had authorized the requested increase for the Associate Director, but an increase of only one thousand for me, the Director.

We were all dumbfounded, Claude Bissell not least. I could imagine no reason for the Prime Minister's action. True, I had been appointed by a Liberal government, but I had never taken any part in politics, and could as well have been thought a Conservative: all our family in the Maritimes were Tories. There had not been, and could not have been, any accusation that the Council, or I as Director, had ever been influenced by political considerations in the recommendation or making of grants and scholarships. I had the full confidence of the Council. The money required for my salary increase was the Council's own money: it did not have to come from or be passed by the Treasury Board. I simply couldn't understand why the Prime Minister had made this invidious distinction between Bussière and me.

The explanation, when it came, was astounding. When Douglas Weldon took over the chairmanship of the Council, at the expiration of Claude's time, he, like Claude, came to me to discuss my salary, expressing his dissatisfaction, indeed indignation, at my treatment. He told me that he was asking Claude Bissell to write again to the Prime Minister, urging the recommended increase. He himself, he said, was going to see Mr. Diefenbaker personally. "As a matter of fact," he said, "I have already talked with him about the matter." He looked me straight in the eye, and as nearly as I can recall his words, he told me: "Mr. Diefenbaker said, 'Trueman's a Grit, and his son Peter's a Grit, and writes columns in the Montreal *Star* criticizing me and my government. Why should I raise Trueman's salary?'"

Some time later the Liberals returned to power, and Doug Weldon, a Conservative of Conservatives, promptly went to Mike Pearson, and with no difficulty secured his authorization for my salary to be raised by four thousand dollars. I was happy about that, but the unhappy fact remains that Diefenbaker's malice kept my superannuation allowance far below the figure I should have had. For the head of our nation's government to defy the unanimous recommendation of the Council in order to vent his personal spite on an individual whom he could not criticize on professional grounds is an act that indicates smallness of mind, and other unpleasant qualities besides.

In those early days of the Canada Council's existence its power to sustain and influence for good the arts, humanities, and social sciences was pathetically less than it is now. The last time I checked the figures, I learned that the Council had spent, on all its programs, approximately eighty million dollars within its last fiscal year. In my time, rather less than three and a half million was our greatest annual revenue, roughly 4½ per cent of what the Council has now, or what it had two or three years ago, before the government created a separate council for the social sciences and humanities. I don't mean to suggest that this income was negligible. But it was quite clear that we had to walk delicately. We could not launch vast and elaborate schemes to help huge numbers of scholars, artists, writers, performers, and organizations: orchestras, ballets, theatres, operas, art galleries, libraries. To be sensitively selective, just, and consistent with Council policy in the recommendations that I put forward – supported, of course, by Bussière and Dwyer – was a task that often required a cunning and a subtlety that I sometimes felt I didn't have. I quote from the Council's first annual report:

To get good value The Canada Council will have to exercise every device of philanthropic leverage – matching grants, teaching the teachers, multiplying the results of successful experience, backing success – thus encouraging others – and singling out and emphasizing by every means the importance of creative talent.

One permanent objective in the interest of our national well-being must be to increase the recognition, the prestige and the powers conferred on the scholar and the creative worker. Upon them largely depend the quality of our people and the image we have of our country.

I suspect that the statement in that last sentence does not represent a majority opinion in our country, or, indeed, in anyone's country. But I believe that the place Canada will have in history, and the image that we and others will have of her, will not depend on the statistics of our grain trade, on the balance of our imports and exports, on the magnitude of our agricultural, forest, and mining production, or on the reputation of any Minister of Finance, but in large degree on the books we write, the pictures we paint, the films we make, the music we compose, the buildings and statues we erect, and on the extent to which we are able to raise, on a broad front, the level of the national culture, using that word in its widest sense.

There can't be any doubt that the Canada Council has been an enormous influence for good so far as the scholars and the creative workers are concerned, whether as individuals working alone or as belonging to an organization. Contrasting the state of the arts in Canada twenty years ago with the present makes clear two facts. First, remarkable advances have been made both in quantity and quality of production, in both the creative and performing branches. The terms "creative" and "performing" are useful in any discussion of the arts, but I think that the line between them can't be clearly drawn. There is creativity in the fine performance of a symphony, of a play, of an opera, of a ballet, of a song. I think it is Northrop Frye who makes the point that a student reading a piece of literature with comprehension and sensitivity is performing a creative act. What else can you call the remarkable feat – and it *is* remarkable when you come to think of it – of creating life and emotion and significant meaning out of black marks on a white page? Second, the Canada Council has been a great force in bringing about these advances.

In the third annual report, I wrote, "The Council's terms of reference ensure that its activities will be concerned almost exclusively with that which cannot be weighed on the scales, measured by the foot-rule, or calculated with the assistance of the tables at the back of the book." This is certainly true. It is also true that the Council was created at a time when already the country was beginning to have a little more feeling for the importance of the matters which had been made the objects of the Council's concern. Nevertheless, there are *some* measurements which support the view that the Council has exerted a profound influence: the increase, for example, in attendance at symphony concerts given by orchestras that have received substantial and continued support from the Council; the increase in numbers of concerts given with the assistance of the Council; the wider diffusion of arts activities, stimulated by Council grants; that is to say, the greater numbers of Canadians, in their own communities, who hear good music by orchestras and choirs, and see art exhibitions; the greater amounts of money raised locally in support of the arts, as a direct result of stimulating grants made by the Council; the great increase in the purchase of works of art by the government and by the public; and so on and on.

The Council of course has made mistakes. But that fact – and I'm sure it is a fact – is by no means always easy to prove. A grant to an individual who shows promise of becoming a "successful" painter, concert pianist, actor, singer or whatever, is a gamble. In many instances, eventually there will be adequate proof that the gamble was wise; the protégé will become a painter of note, a concert pianist of distinction, a leading soprano in our National Opera, or at Covent Garden. But in some instances he or she will not. Has the Council's money, then, been wasted? I always maintained that you couldn't possibly tell. In the first place, the continuing education and training of a large number of Canadians who are concerned for the arts is a useful contribution to the quality of the national life, even if not all of them make careers of great distinction. In the second place, there is no way of knowing what the influence will be, in their communities, of individuals of this type: the stimulus they may give as teachers, as fine local performers, as members of committees that try to do something for the arts; the chance that some pupil next in line, so to speak, stimulated and trained by a teacher of a much higher standard than was formerly available, may prove to be a successful gamble for the Council, largely because of that first and supposedly unsuccessful gamble that was made on his teacher. In other words, I should think that almost every Council grant has a good chance of making itself felt beneficially, either by helping individuals or organizations to achieve distinction, or by raising, however slightly, the national level of concern for excellence in some area of the Council's responsibility. And what I have contended here about the arts is also true of the humanities and the social sciences.

One of the most interesting problems the Council had to face was the proper disposal of the University Capital Grants fund, the fifty million dollars to be given to universities to help them in their building programs. Very early the Council received urgent representations from the universities that whatever else we included in the list of eligible buildings, we should include student residences. The Council agreed. But Max Henderson, the Auditor General, argued that under the provisions of the Canada Council Act we were not legally entitled to grant money for this particular purpose. I have a great admiration and liking for Max Henderson, but it is my opinion that now and then he stepped over the boundaries of his proper function, and involved himself in questions of policy which he should have avoided. The Council was united in its opinion that the building of proper halls of residence was legitimately a part of our responsibility to support the arts, humanities, and social sciences. I, as an academic and former university president, was convinced that the nature and function of the residence fell clearly within the scope of our responsibilities, and I thought, too, that I knew a lot more about university education than Max did. We were supported in our view by an impressive body of university opinion ranging from statements made by the Massachusetts Institute of Technology, to those of the University Grants Commission in Britain. One argument that was hurled against us was that science students would no doubt occupy space in many of these residences, and that the Council had no mandate to do anything for the sciences with funds initially supplied by the government. However, we won our argument and were able to continue the distribution of money to the universities for halls of residences, which after all make up only a small proportion of their building programs.

All the universities we consulted were persuaded that the nine-to-four student, who arrived from the outside in the morning and vanished into the outside in the afternoon, was not realizing the fundamental values inherent in the proper concept of university education. And with that opinion my own experience, as student, teacher, and administrator, compels me to agree. In my undergraduate days at Mount Allison, where I spent three years in residence, "the bull session" – I don't know what it's called now – was by no means the least important element in the educational process: to argue, to learn with astonishment the wrong-headed opinions of others, to be forced to correct one's attitude, to learn to concede defeat with good temper, and to triumph without exultation, to discover that wit and intelligence are not confined to the "big men on campus," to be directed to books and customs and manners of which one had been ignorant, to rejoice in the companionship of far-into-the-night, wholly unparliamentary sittings – all these, I am convinced, were invaluable "educational" experiences of the humane variety, impossible to come by in the lecture hall, more lasting than much formal instruction.

But now I must record, with dismay, that the Federal Government has executed its plan for the dismemberment of the Canada Council. The social sciences and the humanities have now been united in a separate organization known as the SSHRC. It is widely accepted that the original impulse to give them an independent research agency came chiefly from the social scientists, who apparently believed that their needs would be more generously met by government, and their programs more freely planned and implemented, if considered apart from the claims of artists, musicians, actors, and dancers. But the new Council will be under the close scrutiny and direction of the Federal Government: in the Social Sciences and Humanities Research Council Act, the Council is required "to advise the Minister in respect of *such matters relating to research as the Minister may refer to the Council for consideration.*" [5(1)(b)] The by-laws of the Council "for the regulation of its proceedings and generally for the conduct of its activities including the establishment of special,

156

standing, or other committees of the Council" must be made "Subject to the approval of the Governor in Council." [14(1)] The Council's appointment of its officers must be made "with the approval of the Minister." [15(1)]

These provisions have created a close relationship with the Ministry to which the Council reports, and therefore with the Cabinet, and are already leading to loss of the independence which supposedly the social scientists crave, and to a political determination of the nature and extent of research in the social sciences and the humanities. This determination should be made by professional scholars. It isn't claimed that professional scholars have been given all wisdom in this respect, but their training, their expertise, and their continuing concern for wide-ranging scholarship are far superior to any relevant virtues that may be claimed for politicians – no matter how well-intentioned. To hand over to government the choice of what should be studied, and, by implication, what need *not* be studied, is to entrust direction to those who are far removed from the seats of learning, and upon whom non-scholarly pressures are inevitably brought to bear.

State support for the arts, social sciences and humanities without state control is perfectly possible and unquestionably desirable. The Government is, of course, not without responsibility for the ways in which public money is spent by the Council. But it would have had sufficient authority if it had contented itself with a general statement of the Council's functions, and limited its own powers to the appointment of Council members and the President, who is also the Chief Executive Officer, and to the appropriation of funds. It is a melancholy thought that the new Council's chances of obtaining more money will be in direct proportion to Cabinet approval of its programs. One shudders to think of the consequences for the arts if the Canada Council should be subjected to this type of Cabinet direction. Furthermore, it is a significant cultural loss that desirable interplay among the arts, humanities, and social sciences is now destroyed at the national level.

The object of these two councils ought not to be the planning and implementation of specific programs supposed to meet national needs as defined by a committee of so-called experts – either professional scholars or politicians. The object should be to ensure the constant flow into our society of a broad stream of gifted and industrious men and women, free to engage in whatever artistic or scholarly endeavours they may be drawn to by their training and talents. In this country of free enterprise why not let the market – whether artistic, intellectual, or commercial – determine the direction that the arts and scholarly research should take? The application of this philosophy might result in the temporary omission, here and there, of what ought to be investigated, but the harm done in this way would be slight in comparison with the serious damage that government control will do to the free development of arts, scholarship, and pure research.

CHAPTER EIGHTEEN

At a luncheon in Québec City in 1964, when the Council was having its annual out-of-town meeting, I sat beside Ed Hall, President of the University of Western Ontario, an old friend and colleague since the time when I had assumed the presidency of the University of Manitoba, in 1945. To my surprise, quite abruptly he said, "Bud, I don't know how old you are or how long you want to stay with the Council. But when you're ready to quit, I want first option on your services." The telephone had rung again!

A month or so later I thought, "Why not find out if Ed has anything particular in mind?" I had been at the Council for nearly eight years. The Council's income was increasing very slowly; much too slowly in fact. Too much of my time was being spent on exactly the same old problems, recommending the same old grants, writing the same old letters. "Be frank with yourself, Trueman, you have to admit that the bloom is off the grapes. Failing a sudden, considerable, and wholly improbable increase in Council income, for an expanded range of activities and for trying out new ideas, you are soon going to be bored. Perhaps Ed has a job in mind into which you could hurl yourself with the old excitement, and at the same time get yourself back inside a university, where you'd like to be during your last years of service."

I had learned from my rather peripatetic career two things. One, many men stay too long in the one top administrative position, after the initial excitement has disappeared, after they have shot their bolt, made the particular contribution which is theirs alone to make; and two, there is nothing like a change of occupation to give one a shot in the arm, set the adrenalin flowing: a new location, new colleagues, new friends – even new enemies – new problems to solve, new necessity to explore one's capacity for new action. This was probably the last time the telephone would ever ring to herald an offer of yet another adventure.

I wrote to Ed and caught him at just the right time. The Principal of University College had resigned, and quite unexpectedly, so had the man who was in line to succeed him. Ed proposed that I take over the Principalship of the College, and do some teaching in the Department of English. Ed had always made a wrong estimate of my scholarship: his error was again made evident by his suggestion that I give the Department a hand with its post-graduate students. I had no intention whatever of agreeing to that. I had been away from rigorous study far too long – for twenty-three years – and besides, I had never been a dedicated researcher. I took the post, however, with Ed's agreement that what I might do in the English Department would be determined by discussion between the Head and me.

The Head was John Graham, son of Bill Graham, who was the Principal of United College during my time at the University of Manitoba. John is an excellent man in every way; scholarly, just, and friendly. But I could see reflected in his face, when I first went to talk with him, something of the anxiety which I had expected he would feel. Here was this ex-university president, this administrative type, no doubt of dubious scholarship, inclined to want to run things, who was being forced on the Department by President Hall. What to do with the fellow? I soon relieved his anxiety, however, by assuring him that I had no desire to work with graduate students. My principal scholarly interest, I explained, was in the Elizabethan age in general and Shakespeare in particular; over a great many years I had kept up my reading in that area. I said, "If you have an undergraduate pass course in Shakespeare for which you need an extra teacher, I'm your man. I think I can do a good job for you, and I'd like that post very much." It was almost comical to see the relief which promptly lightened John's face. Apparently I had said exactly the right thing. The pass course in Shakespeare was divided into several sections of thirty or forty students each, and one section lacked its teacher. The job was mine. I was happy, John was relieved, and Ed Hall was satisfied with the arrangement we had made.

But I'm getting ahead of myself. I still haven't cut loose from the Canada Council. About this time we had started negotiations with the federal government for more money. This step was taken not without some serious soul-searching. The difficulty was that as long as we depended entirely for our income on the revenue from the Endowment Fund, which was in the sole possession of the Council, we were independent; the Canada Council Act gave us complete freedom – that is, within its limiting provisions – to decide, with no possibility of outside interference, who should receive scholarships and other types of grants, and for what reasons: if we asked for and received a substantial annual appropriation from Government, we would put the affairs of the Council on the floor of the House, inviting interference from members on behalf of constituents who had seen little or nothing of Canada Council money, or from those Members who might try to force us to alter our policies and our priorities. Would not this very natural development ultimately destroy the Council's cherished independence? Had not the Government been wise, when it drew up the Act, to confer this independence upon us?

It appeared useless to press for a substantial increase of the Endowment Fund. To get in that way the additional income we needed – several million dollars a year – would require a doubling of the Fund; adding another fifty million dollars. No one thought there was the slightest chance of that. It would probably be much easier to persuade the government to give us annual appropriations of, say, three or four million; we would thus leave ourselves free, when necessity arose, to ask for additional sums of these relatively modest proportions. Whatever political risks might reside in this method, the Council decided that it offered the only practical solution of our financial needs.

Between the time when I decided to resign (and had indeed accepted Western's offer) and the date on which my resignation was to take place, the Government, to my considerable surprise, came through with an appropriation of ten million dollars, and left the Council free to spend it in a single year or over as many years as it saw fit. This new prosperity created a curious situation. The last two or three months of my term as Director coincided with annual budget-making time. Clearly, with the new appropriation in hand, we were going to double – *at least* double – our budget for the coming year. Our Minister, Maurice Lamontagne, felt, quite logically, that it would be awkward for my successor to take charge precisely at a time when a new and doubled budget had been adopted, about which he would have had no previous information and in the drafting of which he would have had no chance to exercise his judgment and influence.

The Minister asked me if I would agree to an earlier date for my resignation, thus allowing the earlier appointment of the new Director and giving him a chance to work on the new budget; and if I would continue with the Council until the date originally set for my departure, under a new and short-term appointment as Special Consultant and Adviser, at my existing salary.

I felt that I couldn't refuse to go along with this proposal, but I knew very well that unless everyone understood that my temporary appointment was in reality a sinecure, the scheme wouldn't work. You can't bring a new man into the senior executive and administrative office of a small organization and expect him to be content to have his predecessor immediately at hand, still on the force, and breathing down his neck. By this time Doug Weldon's term of office was ended – Weldon had succeeded Bissell – and a new Chairman had taken over: Jean Martineau, a prominent Montreal lawyer. Jean was an excellent chairman, a polished, charming gentleman; sensitive, experienced, knowledgeable, and sufficiently tough. I went to him with the Minister's proposal, and told him that although I fully understood the reasons that had prompted it, the situation that was being set up was not practical, either for the new Director or for me. Martineau shushed me gently, and said that I would be of inestimable service to my successor, Jean Boucher, during his first months in office. I didn't believe this, but, as I have said, felt that I had to go along with the proposed arrangement. The event proved that I was right. After a week or so in this awkward position, I cleared out, after consulting C.J. Mackenzie, and Jean and I went to Bermuda for a short vacation.

The timing of my departure from the Canada Council was unfortunate in another connection. I had to tell Jean Martineau, the new Chairman, immediately on his arrival, that I was leaving. And then, quite unbeknownst to me, the Associate Director, Eugène Bussière, had also made up his mind that eight years were enough. He resigned at exactly the same time I did, to join the Canadian foreign service as "our man" in Marseilles. So there was Martineau, after only a few weeks in office, confronted with the resignation of his two top executive and administrative officers.

It was something of a blow to the new Council Chairman to lose this experienced and highly capable officer and me, at the same time, and so soon after his assumption of duties. I'm sure he wondered if his appointment and our departure stood in the relation of cause and effect! Nothing could have been further from the truth. When Eugène and I had made our separate decisions to leave, neither of us had known who the new chairman was going to be.

I was very unhappy about this *contretemps*, especially since Martineau proved to be such a good Chairman and such a warm, friendly person, with whom it was easy to get acquainted and to be on the best of terms. Eugène and I went to Montreal to see him before each Council meeting; we were always given his full attention during the hour or more of our consultation: like Claude Bissell, he was scrupulous in this regard. And we very soon found that he brought quick and subtle understanding to the Council's major problems, and clear, sane judgment to its policies and to our proposed responses to the numerous appeals for help. I was able to make him understand that the inconvenient timing of my departure, and of Eugène's, was pure coincidence. In fact, the strongest feelings of regret I had on leaving the Council were occasioned by the breaking off of this new but quickly valued relationship with Jean Martineau.

I had plunged into my London adventure, as I had plunged into the Presidency of the University of Manitoba and the Directorship of the Canada Council, without making any careful enquiry about persons, problems, atmosphere, local peculiarities of outlook and the like. It wouldn't have made any difference if I had poked about in this way, for I was determined to get back inside a university and to do some teaching. I was quite content to dive in and make my discoveries afterwards. I don't boast about this attitude; I simply record it. After all, what would it have profited me to weigh and consider, advance and retreat, hesitate and be bold, before I took the Canada Council job? There wasn't anything I could discover about it, apart from what could be found in the Canada Council Act. My attitude towards the move to Western was a simple repetition of the attitude I had taken to the Canada Council. Perhaps it arose from a conviction that you can't find out anything significant about a new position until you have accepted it and occupied it.

These rather simple reflections remind me of a passage which I underlined some years ago in my copy of Moriae Encomium (In Praise of Folly) by Erasmus (Princeton University Press). In section eleven he writes:

And first, if prudence depends on experience of affairs, to whom does the honor of this attribute belong? To the wise man, who, by reason partly of modesty and partly of faint-heartedness, will attempt no action? Or to the fool, who is not deterred from any enterprise by modesty, of which he is innocent, or by peril, which he never pauses to weigh? The wise man runs to books of the ancients and learns from them a merely verbal shrewdness. The fool arrives at true prudence, if I am not deceived, by addressing himself at once to the business and taking his chances.

So it appears I have found great authority for my approach to these new positions, merely at the cost of placing myself in the ranks of Erasmian fools, a cost which I cheerfully pay.

But one thing about the job I was sure of in advance: it would commit me to teaching undergraduates a course on Shakespeare; and about that I knew I would be excited, and I suspected, although I was not certain, that I would be successful. The only uncertainty I felt about my future performance in the lecture-hall arose from the circumstance that I would be confronting this new generation of students, from whose ranks had emerged what in my quaint old-fashioned way I had been calling agitators, persons disrespectful of what I had always thought properly constituted authority, young men and women dressed in a fashion that I abhorred and still abhor, devotees of rock music, which stuns the listener into a mental and spiritual stupor – at least so I think. Could I control the class? Could I compel its interest? Could I command the respect that, in my opinion, is an indispensable condition of success in teaching? Could I, in fact, understand them, and would they understand me?

When I inspected my quarters at University College, I found I had a huge and magnificent office. I also found – and this has been my consistent good luck – an excellent secretary in the person of Helen Wilson. To my surprise I discovered that I was not the Principal of the College but the Dean. The title had been changed, I was told, because the College principals had come to believe that they were being unfairly out-ranked by the faculty deans, and were conceded less authority and influence than were properly theirs. But they had, nevertheless, enough influence to bring about the change. I myself much preferred the former title, and could not believe that we had achieved higher status simply by dropping one name and assuming another.

The most important thing, for me, was to get to know the academic staff. It was easy to meet the departmental heads, who dropped in to see me, one by one, soon after I took over. The rest of the group I didn't know, but felt I ought to meet as soon as possible. I decided that I must at once call a meeting of the College faculty to give myself a chance to look over the people I was going to work with, and to give them a chance to look over the new Dean. In a confrontation like this there is something of drama. I was not only new in the office, but unknown, I fancy, to most of the faculty. I gathered, too, from certain conversations I had, that practically no one, perhaps no one at all in the College, had been genuinely consulted about my appointment. Certainly no nominating committee had been struck, and no list of "possibles" carefully scrutinized by representatives of those who were to be the new Dean's colleagues. This was in the bad old days when a university president had much more freedom and power than he has now; that was certainly true of Western in 1965. No doubt President Hall had talked about me, as a possible Dean for University College, with a few of his senior cabinet ministers, but I believe consultation went no further than that. I knew, as I faced my faculty, that to most of them I was an unknown, or nearly so, and I sensed some feeling of anxiety and even of resentment arising from my "newness" and from the manner of my appointment, not unlike the feelings that I had seen reflected in John Graham's face as he wondered what to do with this administrator who was being thrust into his Department of English.

Now I was anxious of course to recommend myself to the faculty at the meeting, and I did my very best to put on a good performance. I don't recall much of the brief speech I made before we took up the items of business on the prepared agenda, but I believe I said two things that helped me in this by no means wholly comfortable situation. I informed my hearers that I was engaged to teach a section of the pass course on Shakespeare, explained my interest in teaching, reported that I had already met my class, and that I found myself again confronted by the ancient difficulties that all pedagogues have to face. I told them too that these basic difficulties had never been better stated, in my opinion, than by Dr. Johnson in his *Life of Milton*. Johnson gave sceptical treatment to Milton's reputation as a teacher of unusual skill and achievement. He wrote, "Those who tell or receive these stories should consider that nobody can be taught faster than he can learn. The speed of the horseman must be limited by the power of the horse. Every man, that has ever undertaken to instruct others, can tell what slow advances he has been able to make, and how much patience it requires to recall vagrant inattention, to stimulate sluggish indifference, and to rectify absurd misapprehension." This sort of experience, common to all teachers, would no doubt serve, I assured the faculty, to keep the Dean honest.

The other thing I did that helped me, as far as I could tell then and later, was to suggest that I disliked protracted meetings in which the Chairman failed to exercise control, and allowed discussion to be carried to unnecessary and unreasonable lengths. I promised that if we could have a good attendance at these faculty gatherings, I would undertake to dismiss each meeting at the end of an hour. If at that time important business remained to be discussed, I should still prefer to adjourn, and call another meeting a little later on. The faculty accepted this proposal without dissent, and, I think, with relief.

I kept to the agreement rigidly, and I don't recall any occasion on which we did not get through our agenda by the end of the hour. This was accomplished by clearing away, before the meeting, as much business as could properly be handled in committee, by consultation with department heads, and by carefully keeping off the agenda items not worth the attention of the whole faculty. Even though erosion of the President's and the Dean's authority and influence had already set in, there still were areas in which one could move about unimpeded, and after consultation with senior colleagues, take action, thus avoiding the necessity of making a "big production" of minor issues at a faculty meeting. God knows what the situation is today.

This business of running – if that's the right word – the College was bound to be heavy and time-consuming. I was pleased that the budget contained provision for an assistant to the Dean, but I was dismayed when I learned how small that provision was. Apparently it was assumed by the faculty that one of its junior members, for a modest recompense, would give me a few hours a week, in which he would do I scarcely knew what. This was not at all my idea of an assistant. I had no intention of locking myself into an administrative post that would confine me to a life of committee meetings, paper work, interviews, and long, long office hours. For one thing, I had undertaken to teach a course in Shakespeare, and I was determined to have hours for study and for the careful preparation of lectures. I felt that I was in a pretty strong position, and I had no hesitation in asking for much more substantial help.

I was successful in getting what I wanted, and more than fortunate in securing the services of Ray Allen, well-known campus personality and retired professor of physics. Without Ray, a down-Easter and a Mount Allison graduate, I can't imagine how I could have got through my two years at Western. I worked him hard, but he didn't seem to mind that. He cheerfully took a great deal of responsibility, chiefly in budget preparation and supervision, and in providing me with analyses and statistical reports. All of these he did, and other things too, with great skill and complete integrity.

CHAPTER NINETEEN

It took me only a few lecture-periods to realize that all my fears of a possibly difficult classroom situation had been unwarranted. I got nothing but the most courteous treatment and careful attention from my students, right from the start. There was much, then, to make me happy at the University: my teaching, the excitement of a change in occupation, new colleagues and friends, and the brisk summons to deal with new problems.

But a dark cloud hung over this agreeable scene. I learned that the faculties, especially the faculty of arts, with which I had most to do, were in a state of near revolt against the President and the Board of Governors. I'm not going to analyse and discuss this state of affairs. The circumstances were much the same as those which led to similar deeply felt dissatisfactions in scores of other universities: the form of university government, which had not kept pace with the times, lack of adequate representation by the academics in what is so often termed "the decision-making processes," lack of communication between the Board and the President on the one hand, and the teachers and researchers on the other; a sense on the part of the faculties of being helpless to deal with problems they thought should be dealt with, of there being no recourse to a just and freely accessible court of appeal. And so on. The general history of those disturbed days is well known.

All this put me in a very awkward position, especially the fact that so much resentment and indeed strong animosity were building up against the President, Ed Hall. I was shocked at a general faculty meeting one day, over which Mark Inman, the Vice-President, presided. (He and his wife later became our dear friends.) Mark began the meeting by saying that he had a written message to deliver from the President, and then read it out. I forget what exactly it was, but it was an innocuous statement, making sense, and not intruding on any of the so-called sensitive areas. What shocked me was that Professor Henry Mayo, political scientist, immediately rose to his feet and said, apparently to the satisfaction of the meeting, "Well, ladies and gentlemen, let's not pay any attention to anything that comes from the President." This struck me as unscholarly and grossly discourteous. Scholars don't dismiss an idea because it comes from a certain source: they examine it, and accept it or reject it or qualify it on its merits as an idea. This unpleasant incident served to show me how far the rot had set in, and how hopeless the position was in which Ed now found himself. I wondered, after the meeting, if perhaps I had been guilty of cowardice, in that I hadn't jumped to my feet and protested. But two considerations held me back: I was a very new boy indeed, and I felt it wise to hold my tongue until I understood the situation better, and had got my bearings; and I was an old friend of the President who, as I'm sure many people knew, had almost single-handedly brought me to the University; anything I might have said would have been taken as an indication that I would prove a reactionary – a rôle that I was by no means disposed to assume.

The faculty association became increasingly aggressive and at times, I thought, unreasonable and unfair in its tactics. But nevertheless there were indeed reforms that cried out to be made. For instance, the Senate had far too many non-academic members: town officials, business men, reeves. Academic representation was ridiculously small. A university senate ought surely to be essentially an academic body, since the matters it deals with are academic in their nature: when they are not directly so, then they are so in their basic implications. There was no faculty representation on the governing body; the logic and necessity of such representation had never been evident to the majority of the governors. The University Act was out of date in these respects and in many others. I recall that the Board came to the conclusion, rather suddenly I thought, that there was need for some measure of Senate reform. I received a letter authorizing, indeed asking, University College to present its views of the matter. (The same letter was of course sent to the other colleges and to the faculties.) I placed the document before a college faculty meeting, expressed with some vigour my own opinion of the present Senate structure and said, in effect, "Here's our chance. We mustn't lose the opportunity to make the Senate an academic body, as it should be. Let's pull no punches!" With some enthusiasm we appointed a drafting committee and instructed it to make its report as soon as possible. I was astonished and, I confess, pleased when after the meeting, one of the younger of my faculty members said to me in the hall, "What an old fire-eater you are! Who'd have guessed it?" I was even more pleased by this than I was by another remark made to me by another faculty member one day when I was wearing a dark top-coat and a floppy black felt hat: "You look positively like a pirate, Mr. Dean, as you move along the corridor!" Pirate! Fire-eater! *Me?* How delightful!

The decision to let the campus present its views on the Senate was followed almost immediately by examination of the entire University Act. Into this examination everyone and his wife entered with gusto. And about then I observed what was to me a startling development. It became apparent that the Board was parting company with the President. That is to say, suspicious as most members of the Board were of faculty aspirations to a greater share in University government, they began to see that the faculties were not going to be held back; they began to read the signs of the times. But to Ed Hall this faculty attitude or bias, or drive – I can't bring myself to call it a revolution – was anathema. He could not countenance it; he seemed to have little or no disposition to accommodate to things as they inevitably were going to be. He fought with every weapon in his power, chiefly delay and ambiguous response; and the faculty association, so badly had his relations with it deteriorated, even accused him of trickery and deceit – a harsh judgment in my opinion.

Just about the time when I began to sense the Governors' new direction, Doug Weldon, a member of the Board, came to see me in my office. He wanted me to go with him on a visit to the Chairman. The Chairman was Albert Shepherd, a brilliant London lawyer, deeply interested in the University, much concerned for its welfare, and wanting, I'm convinced, to see the Board ride out the storm and make at least whatever minimum accommodation might be necessary to keep hostilities from growing more and more dangerous. Shepherd was a conservative in politics, I imagine, and certainly in his general outlook on society. The "smart" saying that went about the campus at this time was that on most issues the Chairman stood somewhat to the right of George the Third – a gross exaggeration, if I ever heard one; but he was certainly conservative nevertheless, and not in sympathy with the "new thought" of the faculties or with the "new morality" of the students. Both he and Weldon were much distressed by the obvious hostility that had built up against the President, and apprehensive of its possible consequences. They wanted me, as a newcomer, as one not tied into any faction, as a former University president, to give them, in strict confidence, my analysis and judgment of the situation. What was I to do? I began by saying "Look here! I didn't come to Western to stick a knife in the back of my old friend Ed Hall. You're putting me in a damned difficult position." They assured me that they perfectly understood my natural, creditable, and beautiful feelings; but the situation was too unhappy, they said, and even too dangerous for any of us to be over-nice in our response to it.

Confronted by these two vigorous and concerned men, it was impossible for me to keep silent. I refused to tell them what I thought ought to be done, but I could not, I felt, conceal facts from them. I told them of the Mayo incident at the faculty meeting, when it had become evident that distrust of the President had gone so far among so many that anything emanating from his office was tainted by its source. I told them that the extent of this distrust was, in my opinion, both unreasonable and unfair. However, there it was. I told them that I understood, with great sympathy, the feelings Ed must have as he watched the development of faculty determination to change the principles of University government and to move in on the presidential office, and the Board of Governors. All this was contrary to Ed's convictions and long practice, and it was regarded by him as ruinous. Something like a stalemate had been brought about, for the time being. But in my judgment, I said, something would soon have to give, and it was my guess that the giving would not take the form of retreat by a faculty. It was useless to hope that the faculties were going to look back over and remember with gratitude Ed's long and remarkable career of service, invaluable service, to Western. Feelings were running too high for any such consideration to be a mitigating influence on the all-out determination of the faculties to bring about a new form of university government. What precisely the Board ought to do under these painful circumstances was not for me to say, but I suggested that the Board would be wise to prepare itself for change. It was not an easy conversation.

I had hoped that it would be possible for me to stay out of the conflict, and certainly to avoid any personal confrontation with Ed.

On the whole, I managed pretty well. But I was forced to take issue with him on one important matter. A new college, Talbot, was being built. The President's plan was to give it exactly the same constitution as that of University College and Middlesex College. These were strictly arts colleges, teaching no science whatever. Ed was trying to work out a conception which he based on his understanding – his incomplete understanding, I believe – of Oxford and Cambridge. The colleges, while being constituent parts of the University, were designed to be self-contained units, each having its distinctive identity, each commanding its own loyalties and engaging in friendly and fruitful competition with the other. But two circumstances were obviously defeating this scheme: the colleges were not residential, but were simply buildings containing offices, classrooms, an auditorium, and, in Middlesex, a cafeteria; the academic program that each maintained was only partial: neither University nor Middlesex supported all the arts departments, and yet they ran parallel or duplicate departments, most notably, English and History. Not being residential and not being able to meet all the academic needs of its members, each college found that control of its students was only partial, and that the students' association with the college was only, so to speak, fragmentary. The consequence was that the students had almost no sense of identity with the Colleges where they were nominally registered, and no more than superficial loyalty to them. I remember talking with an attractive young woman whom I had not seen before, and learning with surprise that she was a member of University College. "Oh yes," she said with a smile, "I'm a member of University, but I take all my arts classes at Middlesex. Now and then, as I cross the campus, I walk through University, just to remind myself that it *is* my College." (I'm not referring here to Huron, King's, and Brescia Colleges, which were Church institutions, and residential.)

The development that brought me into confrontation with the President was his decision to put yet a third Department of English in the new Talbot College. My people, and some from Middlesex, including its excellent Dean and my good friend, Bob Shervill, came to me in something very like desperation. It was bad enough, they thought, to try to run the two departments in University and Middlesex, but to create a third one on the campus would be a disaster. Neither of the existing departments gave, or could give, all the courses that a full curriculum of English studies demanded. Co-operation in planning their offerings was sought but not always easily found or maintained. There was bound to be rivalry at budget time. Each department kept its eye closely on the financial requests of the other. Items were adjusted down or up in each budget if it was detected that one department was getting ahead of or falling behind its rival. Unlike Huron and King's, the Colleges had no financial resources of their own; every penny they spent had to come from the University treasury. Under these conditions, students flitted back and forth between colleges, getting a little here, a little there, and going for science to the University faculty, which was quite outside the jurisdiction of the colleges.

Having spent a year trying to make sense of this impractical scheme, I was in entire agreement with my unhappy professors that a third English Department at Talbot was unthinkable. There was nothing for it but to compose a lengthy document for the President's eye. As tactfully and reasonably as I could, I put the case for confining English Studies to University and Middlesex. I am happy to say that the President gave in, and we were spared the further multiplication of staff, of rivalries, of discontents, and of inefficiencies, under which we already suffered.

This was the first time that I had in any way bucked the President. I admit that I was uncomfortable about doing it, and I wondered if he would resent my attempted interference with his plans, and if our long and easy friendship would be destroyed. To give Ed all credit, I detected no resentment on his part. I learned that senior administrators often referred to faculty members, including Deans, who did not identify themselves with the movement for change, as being "on the team." The expression suggested to me what Ed and the Board must have been feeling. They had been running a tight ship for years. Cooperation had been the key to progress. Everyone pulled his weight. Everyone was on the team. (There must have been a few, negligible exceptions.) Now a quite different attitude had sprung up on the campus. It was bad enough to learn of widespread dissent among the rank and file, but it must have been painfully disillusioning, even shattering, to learn that departmental heads and deans were capable of assaulting the powers that be. Or should I say, the powers that always had been? I wondered if Ed had said to himself, after my protest against the creation of a third English department, "I always thought that Bud was on the team." This expression revealed, so I thought, two reasons why the Board and the President were finding it difficult to understand the faculties and to make satisfactory

173

progress in the settlement of differences: lack of power to accommodate themselves to new modes of thinking, non-team-like thinking, about university government; and a continuing suspicion that strong disagreement with what had always been the order of things was disloyalty and subversion.

On the other hand I felt that in the disputes that were going on, the faculty association was sometimes too easily and quickly suspicious, and failed to understand the genuine concern of the Board and the President for the welfare of the University, and to take account of the devotion and hard work that they were putting into their respective rôles. On the President's advisory council I heard reports of the intransigence and unfairness of the faculty association; from my professional colleagues I heard of the stubborn and sometimes not straightforward behaviour, as it was described, of the President and the Governors. For an unhappy period of three or four years the situation was practically a stalemate. How progress was made, how accommodation became possible, how the temperature was lowered from boiling to comfortable summer heat is not for me to say: these desirable developments took place, at least in some measure, after I left, and after Carl Williams had taken over as President.

CHAPTER TWENTY

Once again I have to turn back the clock; back from the date I have reached in this wandering memoir. Before I left the Canada Council in 1965, Brooke Claxton had told me, in secrecy – this must have been in 1957 or 1958 – that the Council was "down" in the will of a very wealthy Canadian for a very substantial sum. He didn't know either the sum or the name of the wealthy Canadian. Shortly after Brooke's death, Donald Byers, the head of a big Montreal legal firm, had telephoned me at the Council and asked me to come to Montreal for a chat, which I promptly did. He told me a great deal more about this will, but held back, as he was bound to do, the name of his client, although I thought I knew who she was, and somewhat later my guess was confirmed. I should not, I was told, start smacking my lips in anticipation of a benefaction for the Council in the near future: during the lifetime of his client, now identified as Mrs. Dorothy Killam, widow of Izaak Walton Killam, no funds would be made over to us. We would have to wait until her will was probated. But before I left for Western, something occurred that brought an unexpected and welcome change in the Council's fortunes.

Donald Byers told me that Mrs. Killam was anxious to find out, if possible, just how the Council would go about the management and distribution of her money if she decided to endow a large scholarship program. She wanted, I gather, what in other circles might be called "a dry run." Perhaps that's not quite correct: what she wanted was a demonstration, on a very small scale, but making use of live ammunition, that is, cash. She would provide the money for three handsome scholarships for post-graduate work in medicine and engineering at Dalhousie and the University of Alberta. It was up to me to find the scholars.

I took this matter very seriously. I had to. Here was a chance for the Council to do its stuff, recommend itself as a worthy recipient of unimagined riches. I flew at once to Dalhousie, where I talked with the appropriate people, keeping faith with Mr. Byers by suppressing Mrs. Killam's name, but letting them know as much as I could of the issues that might well hang on our selection of the scholars. I got two names there. I then flew to Edmonton where I repeated my performance, and got the third name. The three young men, two medicos and an engineer, were given scholarships. I kept in touch with the officials at Dal and Alberta, and saw to it that reports were made to Donald Byers (and to Mrs. Killam) on the work of the scholars, which, praise the Lord!, was consistently excellent. Mrs. Killam was greatly pleased by this little demonstration, I judge, as events proved.

A short while after the trial scholarships had been set up, Mrs. Killam began the liquidation of a company, or companies, which she owned, estimating that the capital return from the process, which would take a few years to complete, would be very nearly nine million dollars. Now, after Mrs. Killam's death, her fortune proved to be ninety-three or four million. She certainly didn't stand in need of the cash addition of nine million dollars to what she already held. She asked, Byers told me, "Donald, what *shall* I do with all this money?"

Most of us, I fancy, would suffer no particular perplexity if such a sum were suddenly put in our possession. But if one already has a fortune of some ninety million, it may not be immediately obvious how to dispose of such a conspicuous augmentation of one's wealth. One sympathizes, does one not? Donald Byers, bless his heart, suggested that she divide it equally, as it was realized, between Dalhousie University and the Canada Council. Apparently without demur, Mrs. Killam accepted this solution of her interesting difficulty. Before I resigned from the Council, large instalment payments on the Council's share, estimated to be nearly four and a half million, began to arrive in my office. The first cheque was for well over a million. So, after all, we received money from Mrs. Killam during her lifetime, contrary to her first intent. I like to think that the Council's recommendations and its treatment of the three scholarships had something to do with her change of mind and, subsequently, with the generous provision she made in her will, for a considerable program of permanent Canada Council-Killam scholarships – a program that embraces almost every discipline, with the exception of the Arts as defined in The Canada Council Act.

During my first years at Western, Mrs. Killam died. Donald Byers wrote to me, outlining some of the first steps to be taken in the implementation of the Killam will as it affected the Council, four universities, and the Montreal Neurological Institute, and asking me a question or two. Among the interesting things he had to tell me was that someone – I believe it was Larry MacKenzie – had advised the Trustees to appoint a consultant-assistant; perhaps some retired university president, who could give them necessary counsel on academic matters, and provide the liaison that was clearly going to be needed between the Trustees and the institutional beneficiaries named in the will. Since I had made up my mind not to stay at Western after the normal retirement age of sixty-five – and when Donald Byers wrote to me about the will I was sixty-four – I jumped at the chance to recommend myself most cordially for the post of consultant-assistant to the Trustees, provided they could wait a year before I took over. Consider: I had worked with Donald Byers on the three trial scholarships; I was familiar with the circumstances under which Mrs. Killam had decided to give the Council a very considerable sum during her lifetime; and I had pretty wide and varied experience of universities, and, at the Canada Council, had been accustomed to awarding scholarships. To my great satisfaction, Donald at once wrote me a letter accepting my proposal. He suggested that I go on strength at once, give what counsel and assistance I could during my last academic year with Western, and set up a modest office in Ottawa when I returned in July of 1967. Furthermore, he proposed a generous remuneration for this interim period, on the understanding that it would be substantially increased when I left the University and could give more time to these new duties.

Perhaps this is as good a time as any to say something about Donald Byers. I don't believe that I have ever worked for or with anyone who exceeded him in ability, fairness, generosity, geniality, and the determination to make things go. By "make things go" I don't refer to razzle-dazzle, high pressure, get-out-there-and-get-'em tactics. I am thinking of the detailed provisions of Dorothy Killam's will as they relate to the Canada Council, Dalhousie University, the Universities of Alberta, Calgary, and British Columbia, and the Montreal Neurological Institute, and of the judgment and tact that would be necessary for the successful handling of problems that were bound to arise. The will is an admirable document, surely one of the most enlightened pieces of philanthropy ever probated in Canada. It is a very competent piece of work, in which the conditions under which the Killam Trust funds – for they *are trust* funds – must be held and used are, as one would expect, spelled out with great precision. I'm not going to give details; it is enough to say that permanent association between the six institutions and the Trustees is provided for. Each side, if I may put it that way, will continue, *in perpetuity*, to need to know and take account of the proceedings and views of the other, and of course keep to the terms of the will.

From the start Donald Byers took the stand that this considerable scheme, involving approximately thirty million dollars, must be made to work, and that making it work for the achievement of Mrs. Killam's purposes is by far the most important thing that he and the other Trustees, and I, had to accomplish. To that end he has always been prepared to be sympathetic and tolerant. The nature of this splendid benefaction is such that mere book-keeping, formally distributing the funds, and receiving financial reports from the beneficiaries are not enough. "Let us not," he seems to say, "throw road blocks in the way of the six institutions; if the practical working out of the provisions in the will requires a little accommodation here, a little relaxation of legal rigidity there, all right; let us accommodate, let us relax." I am not suggesting that the Trustees will tolerate any violation of the terms of the will. Not at all! I can only say that it's a superb piece of good fortune for the institutions and, as it happens, for me, that Donald Byers was the lawyer to whom Mrs. Killam entrusted her affairs, particularly the drafting of her will, and is now her principal trustee. She was equally happy in her choice of the other three trustees: Arnold Hart, President of the Bank of Montreal; Conrad Harrington, President of the Royal Trust; and General E.C. Plow, former Lieutenant-Governor of Nova Scotia. Although all are very busy men, they have given, in my judgment, an astonishing amount of time to the affairs of the Killam Trusts.

Among the questions that Donald asked me, in the letter I've referred to, was what my views were about the Trustees' proposed division of the gross sum available for these Killam trust funds. The will authorized the Trustees, within certain limitations, to determine what each of the six institutions should receive. Their first proposal was that the Council should be given 25 per cent. I, who had been

178

the Council's first Director, was naturally keen to have its endowments increased substantially. I wrote back that in view of the national scope of the Council's responsibilities and the great importance of what it was doing for the arts, humanities, and social sciences across the length and breadth of Canada, I thought it should get 50 per cent. After a week or so I had a reply from Donald in which he said that the Trustees took my point, but felt that they couldn't go quite as far as I had proposed, and had settled on 40 per cent. I doubt if the Council ever realized that I exercised at least a modest influence in securing a total increase in its share of the Killam benefactions of nearly nine million dollars.

Before I left Western, Doug Weldon came to me, and said with characteristic generosity that in view of the rather low salary which I had been paid – I had taken a cut of $3,000 a year when I became Dean of University College – he thought I should be given a handsome separation allowance. He put this through the Board, and I got it, although the government bit into it very heavily when I paid my income tax for 1967. With equal generosity, he also said that he thought I should be the next Chancellor of the University, and asked if I would accept the post if the Board made up its mind to offer it. I allowed that I would. The Board made the offer, and somewhat to my astonishment I became a University Chancellor. Some wag among my friends once said to me, "Albert, you have been everything it's possible to be in a university career, except Dean of Women!" Carl Williams succeeded Ed Hall as President, Ed having retired rather earlier than he had expected to because of poor health.

I talked with Claude Bissell about the Chancellorship and asked him what he thought a Chancellor should do, apart, that is, from presiding at Convocations and doing any other public jobs that naturally fall to the office. Claude said that he had been greatly helped by Chancellor Jeanneret at the University of Toronto, because Jeanneret had taken the stand that his principal opportunity of service was to hold up the hands of the President. The Chancellor, senior officer of the University, but non-residential, and non-executive, is *ex officio* a member of the governing body, and it is at meetings of that body that he can support the President most effectively. When you consider that the President stands between, or rather, among, the Board of Governors, the faculties, the student body, and the support staff – and you might add, the Provincial Government – it's not unreasonable to assume that the Chancellor should line up with him, and give whatever help he can as the President tries to deal with the variety of claims made upon him by his besiegers, secure a peace, and survive. This I tried to do for Carl Williams, and I believe I was of some help to him during the four years of my Chancellorship. Jean and I became close friends with Carl and his wife, Peggy, and I developed an increasing regard and admiration for the President as he continued to ride the bucking broncho without being tossed off. And in Carl's early days at Western, when faculty and student unrest was high, and the faculty association was on the warpath, and the University Act was being subjected to close and even resentful scrutiny, for the President to keep his seat and his head was a feat of considerable skill and courage. Despite his promulgation of "Williams' First Law of University Administration: You Can't Win," he won many victories. He is a witty and highly articulate man, who gave the University, in my opinion, sensible, wise, patient, effective, and good-humoured leadership.

As my last year at Western drew to a close, I wrote to Carleton University, notifying the Dean of Arts of my return to Ottawa in July, 1967, and offering my services as a teacher of Shakespeare, or of the literature, especially the drama, of the Elizabethan era. To my surprise and gratification Dean Farr quickly replied that the University was glad to offer me a post of Visiting Professor for 1967-68, and the chance to teach a course in English non-Shakespearean drama, from the beginnings to 1640. I wasted no time in accepting the offer. To teach the non-Shakespearean drama was a challenge. By accepting it, I committed myself to a strenuous bout of book-buying and intense study, much of which, but not all, was review. After a year or so, which I greatly enjoyed, I was switched to the pass course in Shakespeare, which was my first love and much my preference. And for fourteen years, I was a Visiting Professor, somewhat like The Man Who Came to Dinner, and never went home. Who would have believed that after my retirement in 1967, I could still be working at two jobs that I love: teaching at Carleton, and assisting the Trustees of the Dorothy Killam estate? How lucky can a chap be?

When I got back to Ottawa, I found a small office in the Victoria Building, where the Canada Council had first located itself. My luck continued to hold, in that I was able to engage, as a secretary-cum-assistant, Elsie Tudhope, who proved to be another Gladys Yelland, although of widely different personality and background. She had been on the staff of the Canada Council during my time as Director:

Lillian Breen, former Secretary of the Council, recommended her to me. Obviously, Ms. Tudhope's experience of Council affairs has been a considerable advantage in the work of the Killam office. I can't say enough about the excellence of her services. She has kept the records with scrupulous care and accuracy, and has done the necessary "housekeeping" of our small establishment with grace and good nature.

It has been an excitement to have a hand in the operation of the Killam program of scholarships. The program has proved itself of great importance, and my responsibilities in connection with it have kept me in touch with four universities, the Montreal Neurological Institute, and the Canada Council. That association, sustained now for over fourteen years, has given the latter stages of my life a significance and a zest. I have made new and valued friends, from Halifax to Vancouver; academic friends, who receive me with cordiality, and quite outside the sessions of the Killam committees, admit me to their conversation, and keep me alive in the university world, which for me is the best and most beloved of all societies. It is evident, I'm sure, from what I have written about Donald Byers that my relations with him and with the other Killam trustees, have been cordial and inspiriting.

As for Carleton, I can feel nothing but gratitude to the University. It was a specially pleasant circumstance that my long period of service began under Davidson Dunton, who brought to the office of President those remarkable qualities of judgment, foresight, and administrative skill that I had so much admired in him as Chairman of the CBC. At my age I could not have expected to have continued, as I did, in my part-time post, for so many years. It is not only lecturing to the students, the discussions with them in my office, and the letters I receive every year from former members of my class who are prompted to write out of kindness, or good will, or gratitude, that have made those years at Carleton memorable and precious. I think of the men and women I have come to know and have met for conversations, most frequently at the noon-hour in the Faculty Club. It is a temptation to name them and pay tribute to each one. But where to stop? I am deeply indebted to them for companionship, inspiration, and much laughter. They will know whom I mean.

At the end of the last three or four winter terms I had said to myself: "Now, Trueman, you've surely had it! Young, brand-new Ph.D.'s are looking for jobs. About now someone is going to say to the Head of the Department, 'Look here! Trueman has been carried for six or seven years beyond the normal retirement age. He's a nice old boy, and they say he teaches well. (I hope they say this!) But fair is fair: he's had his time and much, much more. Don't you think we should let him go and open up his place to a young man?" I couldn't have found it in my heart to resent treatment of that kind. But, miraculously, the Department kept me on. It was not until May of 1981 that I came to the end of my period of service at the University. As I have already said, I feel nothing but gratitude, and some astonishment, when I think of my days at Carleton.

CHAPTER TWENTY-ONE

This chapter is by way of Epilogue. "Epilogue" is defined in the literary handbooks as a concluding statement, an appendix to a composition. In dramatic usage it is generally applied to the final remarks of an actor who addresses the audience after the performance is over, sometimes referring humbly to the deficiencies of the piece, and asking for kindly judgment and applause.

I have re-read these chapters with care. I find in them omissions which it is too late to make up, and inclusions which it is too late to delete – which is not to say that I haven't performed many necessary acts of major surgery. I turn again to that fountain of wisdom and humanity and superb English prose, Dr. Samuel Johnson. In his wonderful travel book, *A Journey to the Western Islands,* he confesses that he has included much that his readers may think trivial. But he has his beautifully reasoned defence:

> These diminutive observations seem to take away something from the dignity of writing, and therefore are never annunciated but with hesitation, and a little fear of abasement and contempt. But it must be remembered that life consists not of a series of illustrious actions or elegant enjoyments; the greater part of our time passes in compliance with necessities, in the performance of daily duties, in the removal of small inconveniences, in the procurement of petty pleasures; and we are well or ill at ease as the main stream of life glides on smoothly, or is ruffled by small obstacles and frequent interruption.

So much, then, for the omissions and inclusions and trivia in this *my* travel book. I recall that more than once I have turned back to a famous writer – Dr. Johnson, Kinglake, Erasmus, and others – for comforting corroboration of an idea. The old familiar difficulty of

183

being honest confronts me again. Is the author to whom I have turned merely the welcome corroborator of an opinion held, or is he in fact the source of it? I have read in the voluminous works of Dr. Johnson repeatedly – I might say habitually – over a great many years. Professor Tweedie gave me my copy of Kinglake's *Eothen* when I was his young assistant professor at Mount Allison forty years ago. Did I derive ideas and opinions from these writers, make them my own, and then forget to whom I owed the debt? I suspect that this may very well be true, but for the life of me, I can't be sure about it in any single instance.

Although my stream of life has not glided on with unruffled smoothness, its obstacles have been small, and its interruptions infrequent. As I look back over the record, I find judgments which I am already disposed to question, and sentiments which I suspect are inaccurately and perhaps dishonestly reported. I shall let them stand. Of only a few judgments and sentiments can I be certain. And outstanding among them are my conviction that life has been good to me, and a strong feeling, as I began by saying, that I have been a very, very lucky man. In *The Art of Poetry* Horace writes, "The rising tide of years brings many a joy,/ The ebb removes as many." I am happy that the rising tide of years brought me so many joys, and grateful that the ebb has removed so few. One final anecdote will enable me most fittingly to illustrate these sentiments and convictions.

Some years ago, when I was Director of the Canada Council, the Council held one of its annual out-of-Ottawa meetings in Charlotte-town, Prince Edward Island. When we arrived at the airport – a party of, say twenty-five – we were met by a small fleet of taxi-cabs, generously provided by the Provincial Government. The same driver who drove Father Lévesque, Madame Paradis, myself and one other Council member, whose name I have mislaid, to the hotel, drove us, the same four, to the Confederation Building for our morning session. The same driver drove us somewhere for lunch and then to the hotel. He picked us up after we had changed, for we were taking the afternoon off, and drove us to the seashore. Father Lévesque, in a mood of euphoria, lifted up his voice in song. Madame Paradis contributed a clear, pleasing soprano. I threw in an improvised bass. And then, from the driver's seat came a firm, musical tenor part. We were all delighted, and sang our merry way to the seashore, where we saw to it that our musical driver was amply provided with sandwiches and other desirable forms of refreshment. He drove us back to the hotel, and we sang all the way. He drove us to the Premier's house for a buffet supper, and then he drove us to the airport. There, he scrambled out of his seat and hastened to open the rear door for Madame Paradis and the rest of us. As we stood there, collecting ourselves, the driver said, "Well, I dunno about youse guys, but I had a wonderful day."

And as I bring this long account to a close, I can think of nothing more appropriate to say to my family and to my friends and colleagues of half a century, all of whom I thank with a full heart, than, "I dunno about youse guys, but *I* had a wonderful day."